Evora, Portugal

Tourism Environment, a Guide

Author
Albie Fox.

Publisher:
SONITTEC LTD
College House, 2nd
Floor
17 King Edwards
Road,
Ruislip
London
HA4 7AE.

Table of Content

Summary

Travel makes one modest. You got to realize that the world is so big and see what a tiny place you occupy in the world.

With people, their culture, thoughts and ideas also travel. When they go from one place to the other, they are bound to meet people and share their thoughts and experiences with them. This is where exchange of ideas takes place, and it definitely broadens a person's outlook. It makes him/her think in a different way, from a different perspective. When we speak of cultural influences and exchange, food is one of the important factors. The food habits of people say a lot of things about them. It is very interesting to discover new and unknown ways and values; they really add spice to life.

Traveling also creates lifelong memories. Whether a person travels solo or with family and friends, the experience definitely gives him/her nice and exciting stories, which he/she can share with people back home. A good long holiday with loved ones enables him/her to spend some quality time with them, which in turn, helps to renew and restore relationships and creates very strong one-to-one and family bonds. In fact, traveling away from home and spending time with near and dear one(s) can give the relationship an entirely new perspective and possibly, people may start understanding each other in a better way.

Above all, traveling and getting away from our homes enables us to spend some time with our own selves. It makes us more sensitive and more tolerant towards others. It makes it easier for us to meet and mingle with different kinds of people, and also teaches us to live life to the fullest

Evora Introduction to Tourism

Evora is one of Portugal's finest and most delightful towns. It is a true open-air museum with a large number of wonderfully-preserved monuments and buildings of public interest that led UNESCO to protect it as a World Heritage Site.

Each age has left its trace on Evora. It was the Celts who named it Ebora and the Romans gave it its most famous landmark, the Temple of Diana. Dating from the 2nd century, it is one of the Iberian Peninsula's best preserved Roman monuments, raised on a 3m (10ft)-high stone platform, with 14 of the original 18 granite

Corinthian columns still standing. The whitewashed houses, arches, and twisting alleyways that characterize the town reflect the Moorish presence.

The main square, Praça do Giraldo, is the best place to start a visit. It was an execution ground during the Inquisition, but is now filled with shops and cafés, and surrounded by attractive townhouses with wrought-iron balconies. A fountain erected in 1571 in front of the Renaissance Santo Antão Church dominates one end of this spacious square.

From there, the pedestrian Rua 5 de Outubro (lined with souvenir shops) leads to the Roman temple and Loios Convent. The convent is now a splendid pousada but anyone can visit its Gothic church founded in 1485.

The towers of the Sé (cathedral), built in 1186 (and where the flags of Vasco da Gama's ships were blessed before his voyage to India), are seen from here. It is a blend of Romanesque and Gothic, and on the portal are 14th century sculpted Apostles. The Gothic interior has one of the longest naves found in any cathedral in the country, measuring 70m(230ft), and has a large Renaissance organ, thought to be the oldest in Europe. The Gothic cloister with statues of the Evangelists and the Sacred Art Museum are worth seeing. Its most precious item is a 13th century ivory Virgin whose body opens out to reveal intricately carved scenes of her life in nine episodes. Visitors can also climb up to the roof for a view over the town.

Adjacent to the cathedral is the Evora Museum, representing Evora's long history through Roman columns, 16th-century paintings, and modern sculpture. Among the paintings is a 15th-century

Holy Virgin with Child by Alvaro Pires (he is one of the earliest identified Portuguese artists although a number of his paintings are displayed in Pisa and Florence in Italy).

A short walk behind the cathedral leads to the Jesuit University, founded in 1559. It has elegant Renaissance marble cloisters and the classroom entrances are decorated with tile panels representing each of the subjects taught.

A staircase beside the cathedral leads down towards Porta da Moura Square, a picturesque place to rest. It is surrounded by Moorish architecture and has an interesting spherical Renaissance fountain dating from 1556.

As you walk around town you will come across some interesting churches. One of the most eye-catching is Graça Church, a Renaissance building that is unique in the Iberian Peninsula. Built in granite, it has four huge figures supporting globes.

But of all the churches, the one that should not be missed is the Church of São Francisco. It is a Manueline-Gothic structure completed around 1510, and legend has it that Portuguese navigator Gil Vicente is buried in it. Not buried, but on display, are the bones and skulls of some 5000 people covering the walls and columns of the church's Chapel of Bones. The creepiest sight is what looks like the desiccated corpse of a child, hanging off to the right of the entrance, where a sign reads "Nós ossos que aqui estamos, pelos vossos esperamos," meaning "We bones that are here, await yours."

After that, it is a good idea to take a little break in the delightful public gardens near the church, which are also home to the 16th-century Dom

Manuel Palace. Built in Gothic, Manueline, neo-Moorish, and Renaissance styles, it was where Vasco da Gama received his commission to command the fleet that would discover the sea route to India.

Outside the city walls on the road to the train station is Ermita de São Brás ("Hermitage of St. Blaise"), an extraordinary building that looks like a medieval castle, complete with large battlements, gargoyles, and round buttresses. It was built in 1485 in thanksgiving for survival from the plague.

Also outside the walls is the magnificent Silver Water Aqueduct. Walk west from Giraldo Square along Rua do Cano to transverse it and take a look at the houses that were built into its arches.

Around Evora are also numerous prehistoric monuments dozens of sizeable Neolithic menhirs, cromlechs, and dolmens (the one in Zambujeiro, now a national monument, is the largest in Europe, consisting of seven stones, each 6m/20ft high, forming a huge chamber).

The Cromlech of Almendres dating from somewhere between 4000 and 2000 B.C has been called "the Portuguese Stonehenge." It is the most important megalithic group in the Iberian Peninsula, consisting of a huge oval of almost one hundred rounded granite monoliths, some engraved with symbolic markings, assumed to have been used for cult purposes. They have their origins in a culture that flourished in the Iberian Peninsula before spreading north as far as Brittany and Denmark.

A couple of kilometers east is the Cave of Escoural, a cave adorned with charcoal drawings of horses and other animals, the work of Cro-Magnon artists some 15,000 years ago. There are free tours organized on the site.

For more information about these sites, how to get to them, or to book tours, visit the Evora Tourism Office.

One of Evora's restaurants is also famous throughout the country. Apparently O Fialho's excellent traditional dishes are reason enough to drive all the way from Lisbon for dinner.

Evora is less than 2 hours away from Lisbon (there are express buses departing from the Sete Rios terminal), so it is a possible daytrip from the capital. However, it makes an ideal base for touring the Alentejo region and an overnight stay is highly recommended, as the town is especially evocative when floodlit at night.

Evora Outline passage

The Historic Centre of Évora, capital of the Alentejo Province, Portugal, has been shaped by more than twenty centuries of history, going as far back as Celtic times. It fell under Roman domination and still retains, among other ruins, those of the Temple of Diana. During the Visigoth period, the Christian city occupied the surface area surrounded by the Roman wall, which was then reworked. Under Moorish domination, which came to an end in 1165, further improvements were made to the original defensive system as shown by a fortified gate and the remains of the ancient Kasbah. There are a number of buildings from the medieval period, the best known of which is the Cathedral that was completed in the 13th century. But it was in the 15th century, when the Portuguese kings began living in Évora on an increasingly regular basis that Évora's golden age began. At that time, convents and royal palaces sprung up everywhere: St Claire Convent, the royal church and convent of São Francisco, not far from the royal palace of the same name, and Os Lóios Convent with the São João Evangelista Church. These are remarkable monuments that were either entirely new buildings or else constructed within already existing establishments, and which are characterised by the Manueline style that survived in the major creations of the 16th century.

When the University of the Holy Spirit, where the Jesuits taught from 1553 onwards, was established, Évora became Portugal's second city. However, the university's rapid decline began following the expulsion of the Company of Jesus by minister Marquis of Pombal, in 1759.

Évora is also remarkable for reasons other than its monumental heritage related to significant historic events. The 16th century was a time of major urban planning and great intellectual and religious influence. While Évora also has many noteworthy 16th-century patrician houses (Cordovil house, the house of Garcia de Resende), the unique quality of the city arises from the coherence of the minor architecture of the 16th, 17th and 18th centuries. This unity finds its overall expression in the form of numerous low whitewashed houses, decorated with Dutch tiles and wrought-iron balconies and covered with tile roofs or terraces which line narrow streets of medieval configuration and which in other areas bears witness to the concentric growth of the town until the 17th century. It also served to strengthen the fundamental unity of a type of architecture that is perfectly adapted to the climate and the location.

Évora remained mainly undamaged by the great earthquake of 1755 that destroyed many towns in Portugal, including Lisbon. The monuments of the Historic Centre of Évora bear witness to their profound influence on Portuguese architecture in Brazil.

Criterion (ii): The cityscape of the Historic Centre of Évora is a unique place for understanding the influence exerted by Portuguese architecture in Brazil, in sites such as the Historic Centre of Salvador de Bahía.

Criterion (iv): The Historic Centre of Évora is the finest example of a city of the golden age of Portugal after the destruction of Lisbon by the 1755 earthquake.

Integrity

Évora has been inhabited since the 2nd century B.C. During the Middle Ages, it was the royal residence for long periods of time and gained prestige in the 16th century when it was elevated to an ecclesiastical city. Notwithstanding the significant urban changes that occurred through the centuries, Évora still bears testimony to different aesthetic styles.

In spite of the sharp population growth that led to the construction of new quarters to the west, south and east, the Historic Centre of Évora has retained its characteristics within the Vauban-style wall built in the 17th century according to the plans of Nicolas de Langres, a French engineer. Also, the road network that was built around the city walls in the 20th century has contributed to its preservation. Évora's overall integrity has been preserved in terms of both its individual monuments and its townscape. The rural landscape to the north has remained largely unchanged.

Authenticity

Ever since the city walls were classified in 1920 under national law, conservation measures were implemented in accordance with internationally recognised principles. Despite the transformations the city went through in the 20th century, most of its buildings have preserved their structural authenticity and the morphology of the city block has been preserved. Adaptation to modern times has not jeopardized the authenticity of the urban setting.

Protection and management requirements

The Department of the Historic Centre of the Municipality of Évora has the responsibility for over-seeing the implementation of the management plan and monitoring its effectiveness. Its annual working budget comes mostly from the municipality, yet there are several other financial sources such as the Regional Directorate for Culture of the Alentejo and the Directorate General for Cultural Heritage (DGPC).

In order to ensure enforcement of the Law as the basis for the policy and system of rules for protection and enhancement of cultural heritage (Law no. 107 of 8 September 2001), the Decree no. 140 of 15 June 2009 established the legal framework for studies, projects, reports, works or interventions on classified cultural assets. It determined, as a rule, the need for a prior and systematic assessment and monitoring of any works that are likely to affect the property's integrity so as to avoid any disfigurement, dilapidation, and loss of physical features or authenticity. This is ensured by appropriate and strict planning, by qualified staff, of any techniques, methodologies and resources to be used for implementation of works on cultural properties.

According to no. 7, Article 15, Law 107 of 8 September 2001 «Immovable assets considered cultural assets under the World Heritage List shall at all times pertain to the national interest asset inventory for all purposes thereof and within their respective categories».

Similarly, Decree no. 309 of 23 October 2009 equates buffer zones with special protection zones, which benefit from adequate restrictions for the protection and enhancement of cultural properties.

The Municipality of Évora, in cooperation with the national authorities, is studying the modification of the buffer zone of the property that corresponds to the setting of the city, which will be a crucial measure to ensure that the conditions of authenticity and integrity continue to be met

History Layout

From Romans to Moors to Portuguese kings, the proud little town of Évora set amid the cork groves of the Alentejo region, 90 minutes by train or bus from Lisbon has a big history. Évora was once a Roman town (second century B.C. to fourth century A.D.), important because of its wealth of wheat and silver, as well as its location on a trade route to Rome. Most of Évora's Roman past is buried under the houses and hotels of today (often uncovered by accident when plumbing work needs to be done in basements).

The Moors ruled Évora from the 8th to the 12th century. Around the year 1000, Muslim nobles divided the caliphate up into small city-states (like Lisbon), with Évora as this region's capital. And during its glory years (15th–16th centuries), Évora was favored by Portuguese kings, even serving as the home of King João III (1502–1557, Manuel I's son who presided over Portugal's peak of power...and its first decline).

Évora's walled city is compact. The main sights are clustered within a five-minute walk of the main square, Praça do Giraldo. The square had been the town's market during the Moorish period, and to this day, it remains a center of commerce and conviviality for country folk who come to Évora for their weekly shopping. Later it was named for Giraldo the Fearless, the Christian knight who led a surprise attack and retook Évora from the Moors in 1165. As thanks, Giraldo was made governor of the town and the symbol of the city. On this square, all that's left of several centuries of Moorish rule is their artistry, evidenced by the wrought-iron balconies of the buildings that ring the square (and an occasional distinctive Mudejar "keyhole" window throughout the town).

In the 16th century, King João III lived in Évora off and on for 30 years. The town's tourist information office is inside the palace where the king's guests used to stay, but others weren't treated as royally. A fervent proponent of the Inquisition, João was king when its first victims were burned as heretics on this square in 1543.

Until the 16th century, the area behind what's now the tourism office was the Jewish quarter. At the time, it was believed that the Bible prohibited Christians from charging interest for loans. Jews did the moneylending instead, and the streets in the Jewish quarter still bear names related to finance, such as Rua da Moeda (Money Street) and Rua dos Mercadores (Merchants' Street).

Évora's major sights a Roman temple and an early Gothic cathedral crowd close together just off the main square. A lively shopping street connects these sights with the square. Shoppers lag behind, browsing through products of the region: cork (even used to make postcards), tile, leather, ironwork, and Arraiolos rugs (handmade with a distinctive weave in a nearby town).

The Roman temple, with its 14 Corinthian columns, was part of the Roman forum and the main square in the first century A.D. Today, the town's open-air concerts and events are staged here against an evocative temple backdrop. It's beautifully floodlit at night. While known as the Temple of Diana, it was more likely dedicated to the emperor.

Évora's impressive cathedral was built after Giraldo's conquest on the site of the mosque. Inside the cathedral is a 15th-century painted marble statue of a pregnant Mary. It's thought that early priests, hoping to make converts out of Celtic pagans who worshipped mother goddesses, felt they'd have more success if they kept the focus on fertility. Throughout the Alentejo region, there's a deeply felt affinity for this ready-to-produce-a-savior Mary. Loved ones pray here for blessings during difficult deliveries. Across the aisle, a more realistic Renaissance Gabriel, added a century later, comes to tell Mary her baby won't be just any child. The 16th-century pipe organ still works, and the 18th-century high altar is Neoclassical. The muscular Jesus though carved in wood matches the marble all around.

A three-minute walk from the main square is the Church of St. Francis. The saint, who valued simplicity, would likely be horrified by the gilded excess here.

The main attraction at this church is its bone chapel (Capela dos Ossos), just outside the church entrance. The intentionally thought-provoking message above the chapel door translates: "We bones in here wait for yours to join us." Inside the macabre chapel, bones line the walls and a chorus of skulls stares blankly at you from walls and arches. They were unearthed from various Évora churchyards. This was the work of three monks who were concerned about society's values at the time. They thought this would provide Évora, a town noted for its wealth in the early 1600s, with a helpful place to meditate on the transience of material things in the undeniable presence of death.

After reflecting on mortality, it's almost necessary to have a refreshing, cold drink in the pleasant public garden next to the church. Just inside the gate, a statue of Vasco da Gama looks on with excitement as he discovers a little kiosk café nearby selling sandwiches, freshly baked goodies, and drinks. For a quick little lunch, try an *empada de galinha* (tiny chicken pastry) and perhaps a *queijada*(sweet cheese tart a local favorite). The gardens contain an overly restored hunk of the 16th-century Royal Palace. If you look over the stone balustrade behind the palace, you'll gaze out onto a kids' playground and playfields. Life goes on make no bones about it.

The Alentejo region has its own proud cuisine rustic and hearty, with lots of game and robust red wines and Évora's many fine restaurants make this an ideal spot to savor it. While you can sleep and sightsee cheaply here, consider dining royally. Linger over dinner, then, late in the evening, stroll the back streets and ponder life, like the old-timers of Évora seem to do so expertly.

UNESCO World Heritage Status of Evora

Evora is considered world heritage by UNESCO since 1986. The main reason for this distinction is the fact that Evora is the best example of a city in the golden age of Portugal after the destruction of Lisbon in the 1955 earthquake. Evora UNESCO world heritage is a recognition of the city importance and has brought it a lot of visitors over the years. Let´s find out why.

Even people that have lived in Evora for decades still find new details when they walk around the historic centre. Pay attention to what is around you. This way, it will be easy to understand why Evora is world heritage.

Speaking of world, those who have already been to Brazil will find obvious similarities in the architecture of Evora and the ones in cities like

Salvador da Bahia. A little bit of Alentejo in South America.

Évora, UNESCO world heritage city museum

Considered a city museum, Evora has maintained up until today its traditional charm in the whole historic centre inside the Vauban style ramparts built in the 17th century according to a design by the French engineer Nicolas de Langres

But the history of Evora is much older. In fact, in prehistorical times there were already settlements in the region, as it is easily proven by following Evora Megalithic Circuit.

Only much later, twenty centuries ago, the Celts dominated the region. It is thought that one of these tribes, the Eburones (Eburos is a Celtic word for a tree species), were the origin of the name Evora.

During the important Roman domination, Evora came to be called Liberalitas Julia. The Roman Temple was built in this period in one of the highest spots in the city.

Other important peoples in the construction of Evora heritage were the Visigoths, who made alterations to the defensive walls, but also the Moors. These also improved the defences by adding fortified gates and even a kasbah. The Moors' presence is also noted still today in the names of some streets in the Moorish neighbourhood of the historic centre. These names have even survived the Christian reconquest.

A different trace of the past making Evora a world heritage according to UNESCO is the cathedral, the most notable building from the medieval period. Its construction was started in 1186 and finished in the 13th/14th centuries.

However, despite the riches of the past described above, the real golden age of Evora only started in the 15th century, when the Portuguese kings decided to live here most of their time. It was then that a lot of convents and royal palaces were built in Evora, such as Convento de Santa Clara, Convento de São Francisco and Convento dos Loios.

These buildings, built from scratch or on top of old constructions, all have in common the Portuguese Manueline style. This same style would also be used in other 16th century edifices: Palácio dos Condes de Basto; Igreja dos Cavaleiros de Calatrava; Conventos do Carmo, da Graça, de Santo Antão, de Santa Helena do Monte Calvário,...

Actually, the 16th century was very important for Portugal and Evora. Agua da Prata Aqueduct was built in 1537 by Francisco de Arruda. Many of the fountains still existing today were also born during this period. The one in Giraldo Square is the most famous. Evora has also started to have an even greater influence in the country at intelectual and religious levels.

While in the north of Portugal the University of Coimbra played a fundamental role, in the south, that role belonged to the University of Espírito Santo de Évora, where the Jesuits started teaching in 1553. By the 18th century, in 1759, the Marquês de Pombal was determinant in the beginning of the rapid decline of Evora when he expelled the Society of Jesus of the country.

All the monuments and circumstances mentioned so far were relevant towards the distinction of Evora as world heritage by UNESCO. But we can not forget some beautiful important patrician houses like Casa Cordovil and Garcia de Resende's house.

But what makes Evora a truly fascinating and unusual city is the set of small houses of the entire historic centre, essentially built between the 16th and 18th centuries. Painted in white (to reflect the hot Alentejo sun rays), these houses deserve a long walk through the narrow medieval streets.

Only by slowly strolling the tight irregular cobbled streets in the shadow do you get to know the real Evora, in search for iron or tile details.

Travel Guide

The UNESCO World Heritage city of Évora offers many attractions for visitors to enjoy. There is plenty to keep visitors entertained for several days in the city, however if you in Évora for just one day there is a surprising amount that you can see and do.

As Évora has evolved and grown from a small, walled town first established in Roman times, its primary attractions have remained centrally located, clustered mostly in and around the ancient citadel that occupies its highest point, presiding over the maze of winding streets and historic buildings below.

Walking through the streets of Évora is like taking a walk through history. The town is something of a living, breathing museum celebrating Portugal's rich and diverse history of conflicts and conquests, exploration and independence.

Praça Do Giraldo

The lively Praça do Giraldo is the perfect place to start any tour of Évora. The square is flanked on all four sides by a series of historic buildings dating back several centuries, and in some cases more than 2000 years. Here you will come across some of the most impressive examples of Gothic and Romanesque architecture to be found anywhere on the Iberian Peninsula, a collection of ecclesiastical buildings and ancient palaces, clustered around the lovely pedestrianised cobbled central area and fountain.

The Praça do Giraldo is the perfect place to relax over a drink or bite to eat at one of its many cafes and bars. If you are staying in self-catering accommodations or if your hotel does not include breakfast, start your sightseeing day here with a leisurely breakfast in the sun at one of the outdoor tables of the pavement cafes. There is nothing quite like the strong aroma of freshly brewed Brazilian coffee beans and a Portuguese "pastel de nata" (a type of mouth-wateringly delicate custard tart) to get your day of historical explorations off to a flying start.

Temple of Diana

The ruins of the Roman Temple of Diana are located on one edge of the square, dating back some 2000 years to the days when Évora was one of Portugal's most important Roman military outposts. Diana was the goddess of the moon, the hunt and chastity in ancient Rome and the temple was dedicated to her upon its construction in 100AD.

Historians believe that there would have been other similar temples built in the city around the same era, however if this is the case there is little surviving evidence of them now. The Temple of Diana is exceptionally strong, no doubt the reason for its survival as the devastating earthquake of 1755 razed many similar buildings to the ground. The Temple of Diana has had many uses throughout the ages, from execution site during the Inquisition to slaughterhouse in the nineteenth century.

Évora Cathedral

Heading up the square away from the Temple of Diana, you will reach Évora Cathedral, an attractive combination of Gothic and Romanesque architecture. Évora Cathedral is set at the very highest point of the old citadel, in a dominant position presiding over the winding streets of the city below. It boasts an impressive facia of rose granite, which is capped either side by two huge towers dating back to the sixteenth century.

Évora Cathedral is equally impressive inside as it is out. The ornate interior is a study in period opulence, boasting detailed frescoes, impressive sculptures and plenty of pink, black and white marble and stonework. Take a walk through the Gothic cloister to the open terrace to enjoy the sweeping views out across the Alentejo countryside before finishing up in the cathedral's Museum of Sacred Art in the south tower.

Chapel of Bones

Still in the heart of the UNESCO World Heritage site that covers much of the old town, you will arrive at St Francis Church and its famous Chapel of Bones. The St Francis Church is a fine example of late-fifteenth and early-sixteenth century architectural styles. However, its period architecture is not the only reason for visiting the church.

The Chapel of Bones was created by a group of Franciscan monks in an effort to free up some of the surrounding land, which was at the time taken up with no less than 42 different consecrated burial sites. Rather than bury the remains anew, the monks cemented them into the walls of the chapel as a reminder of their own mortality and a place for contemplation and prayer.

There are many other historic attractions to see and enjoy in Évora, many of which, such as the Agua de Prata Aqueduct and the castle walls can be admired simply by wandering through the winding streets of the old town. The Agua de Prata

Aqueduct stretches for nine kilometres from its source right through the centre of town, and is one of Portugal's most impressive architectural works of the sixteenth century, while the old castle walls can be admired at every turn, the perfect reminder of Évora's rich, historic past

Attraction

Temple of Diana

The Temple of Diana is a Roman temple located right in the heart of the historic city of Évora, Portugal. Known in Portugal as the Templo de Diana, the Temple of Diana dates back to the second century AD when Évora was an important Roman military outpost in Portugal, following its heyday as the headquarters of the Roman military commander Quintus Sertorius during the first century BC.

The Temple of Diana is located within the UNESCO World Heritage area of Évora and is one of the city's most important landmarks, and one of the most important pieces of Roman architectural remains in the whole of Portugal.

In ancient Rome, Diana was the goddess of the moon, the hunt and chastity and the temple was dedicated to her upon its construction. It is believed that there would have been other similar temples built in the city around the same time, however if this is the case they have not survived. This example is incredibly sturdy and well built, having sustained little or no direct damage as a result of the devastating earthquake that shook nearby Lisbon to its core in 1755.

Historians have established that the Roman temple was used as an execution site during the

Inquisition and as a slaughterhouse in later years, right up until the late nineteenth century.

The Temple of Diana is located right in Évora's central square at the highest point of the city and is surrounded by a number of other ecclesiastical buildings that were associated with the Inquisition in Portugal during the middle ages. These include the Sé Cathedral, the Palace of the Inquisitor, the Court of the Inquisition, the Palace of the Dukes of Cadaval and the Lois Church and Convent (which has been restored and transformed into a beautiful boutique hotel).

The public library and Évora museum are also located here along with the medieval façade of São João Evangelista and a garden affording lovely views to the Roman aqueduct below and the rolling green hills of the Alentejo countryside beyond.

Considering it dates back more than 2000 years, the Roman temple is in excellent repair, retaining 14 original columns in Corinthian style plus many decorative features in a heady mix of granite and marble.

Agua De Prata Aqueduct

Stretching for an impressive nine kilometres, the Agua de Prata Aqueduct towers over the rooftops of Évora and is a prominent architectural feature no matter where you are.

The Agua de Prata Aqueduct was designed by military architect Francisco de Arruda, architect of the famous Belem tower that stands in the centre of the Tagus River, at the entrance of the Lisbon estuary. It was built upon request of King João III in order to supply water to the city.

Évora's strategic military position was unmatched in this area of central Portugal, but its elevated location and lack of ground water were a problem for this growing town, requiring a solution to bring it from the nearest major supply, some nine kilometres away in the Ribeira do Divor.

The Agua de Prata Aqueduct was constructed over a six-year-period between 1531 and 1537 and is considered to be one of the greatest architectural offerings of the sixteenth century to be found anywhere in Portugal. The northern sections of the project close to the river were relatively quick and easy to construct, mostly running through tunnels, but it was the southern section that meets the town itself that posed the greatest architectural challenges and consequently ended by being so impressive.

The series of arches reaches a height of 26 metres at its peak and cuts its way through the centre of Évora, integrating itself over subsequent centuries to become a part of the town's very fabric. Over the years, houses, shops and other commercial premises have been constructed beneath its arches, the most interesting of these to be found in the area around the Rua do Cano to the far north of town.

The aqueduct originally had its outlet in the Praça do Giraldo, Évora's main square, but was damaged during conflict in the mid seventeenth century. When it was repaired, the team took advantage of the opportunity to move the outlet from the central area to one that had less impact on the day-to-day life and movement of the city.

The Agua de Prata Aqueduct literally means "Aqueduct of Silver Water" and it was named as such for two reasons: the cost, as this was one of Portugal's largest construction projects of the time; and the crystal-clear quality of the waters of the Barragem do Divor and Ribeira do Divor, from which its waters are sourced.

Chapel of Bones

The Chapel of Bones, or Capela dos Ossos, in the Igreja Real de São Francisco in Évora, Portugal, is one of the city's most visited destinations.

The church itself was built in the late fifteenth and early sixteenth century and is a significant sightseeing destination in its own right, thanks to its delightful mixture of Gothic and Manueline architectural styles that were so popular in Portugal at the time. At this time no less than 42 monastic cemeteries were dotted in and around the city of Évora and space was beginning to become an issue, so following the construction of the church a group of Franciscan monks decided to move all the bones to one single, consecrated chapel in order to free up the land for further use and development.

The decision to display the bones rather than hide them away was an interesting one, said to be to provide the monks with the opportunity to contemplate and confront the issue of death readily in one single place.

Hidden Histories

The Chapel of Bones is accessed from the main church via a grand stone arch engraved with the message "the bones here await yours". It is estimated that there are more than 5,000 skeletons covering the walls in the Capela dos Ossos, a mixture of bones and skulls that are cemented into the walls with barely a gap between them. It was believed for some time that the bones were of victims of war or plague but, after further research, it appears that these were simply the mixed remains of the general population of Évora.

In homage to the important role of the church and its monasteries in Portugal, the bones of the monks who built the Chapel of Bones have in fact been kept separate from those that adorn the chapel walls, stored in a white coffin instead. Another point of interest is the two unidentified corpses that are suspended from a wall, one of a grown man and another of an infant boy. No one knows who they belonged to or why they are suspended in the Capela dos Ossos but there are many theories. Perhaps the most popular is that which springs from the sanctity of marriage in Portugal, pointing to the corpses belonging to an adulterous man and his young son.

The Chapel of Bones is one of Évora's more unusual sightseeing destinations, but it is unique and not unattractive, and certainly worth a visit.

Almendres Cromlech

The Almendres Cromlech is a mysterious and enchanting megalithic complex located close to the city of Évora. There are several such complexes to be found elsewhere in Portugal and the Iberian Peninsula, however this is by far the largest, and is in fact one of the primary sites in all of Europe.

The site consists of a number of megalithic structures cromlechs and menhir stones and dates back to between 3000 BC and 4000 BC. Interesting enough, the site was hidden beneath ground and undergrowth for centuries, and was only rediscovered in 1966 when geologist Henrique Leonor Pina was undertaking field work in Évora and the surrounding area.

The site was subsequently fully excavated to expose the full extent of the structures and their complicated chronological history. It appears that the construction took place over a long period dating from the Chalcolithic Age to the Iron Age and it is believed that the site was built either as a religious or ceremonial monument or as a primitive astronomical observatory.

The site of the Almendres Cromlech is reached from the main road leading from Évora to nearby Montemor-o-Novo, close to Guadalupe village. The cromlech itself is located some 1.5 kilometres from the menhir and the two are these days joined by a pedestrian trail set by the local council, which connects these and other megalithic remains that are to be found throughout this rural area of Portugal close to the city of Évora.

The complex is organised into a circle and consists of no fewer than 95 monoliths made of granite, which are in turn organised into smaller groups. The earliest monoliths are smaller and are located towards the western flank of the complex, while those dating from the middle Neolithic and late Neolithic phases spread out to the east where they join the large menhirs.

Archaeologist and historian Mario Varela Gomes established the original layout of the stones from research and rediscovery of their original bases and many have been rebuilt and/or re-erected in their correct positions. Interestingly, the latitudinal position of the complex is around the same as the maximum moon elongation at the time of its latest construction in 1500 BC. Regarding its construction dates, this is also the same at Stonehenge.

The Almendres Cromlech is a delightful and rather ethereal place to wander, explore and discover some of the hidden treasures of the site. Some of the monoliths display carved drawings, hinting at secrets of ancient Portugal that perhaps we shall never discover but which will undoubtedly remain as questions for centuries to come.

St. Francis Church

One of the most famous landmarks in historic Évora, Portugal, is the Igreja de São Francisco, or St Francis Church. Located right in the heart of the UNESCO World Heritage site that covers much of the Old Town, the Igreja de São Francisco was constructed during the late fifteenth and early sixteenth centuries.

The church is perhaps best known as the home of the mysterious (and rather spooky) chapel of bones.

The chapel was the work of a group of Franciscan monks who designed it as a practical solution to the problem of 42 monastic cemeteries taking up too much space in and around the expanding city. They simply moved all the remains from each of the sites and relocated them to one single, consecrated chapel within the church so that the land could be freed up for further use and development.

As for the bones, rather than hiding them away, they took the unusual decision of putting them out on display, cementing the remains of more than 5000 individuals from all walks of life, all over the chapel walls and ceiling.

The chapel of bones may be a must-visit destination on the itinerary of any visitor to Évora, but do not be tempted to overlook the church itself, which deserves much attention in its own right for its lovely gothic and Manueline architecture. Like the nearby Sé Cathedral, the St Francis Church is a vast structure, built on a scale that the guidebooks simply cannot do justice to.

The original design of the Igreja de São Francisco was the work of architect Martim Lourenço, who designed the structure to stand on the site of a former Romanesque church dating back to 1226. There are some lovely Manueline features here, including the grand entrance to the church, which features a design of a pelican and an armillary, emblems of King João II and King Manuel I respectively.

The huge porticos measure some 36x34x24 metres and the large, vaulted nave is the longest of its type to be found in any church in Portugal. The main altar and chance, although dating from slightly different periods, both display some lovely

Renaissance features, while the choir stalls are both entirely different, with one being in classic Renaissance style and the other in opulent Baroque. Twelve open chapels line the sides of the nave, nestled between the main buttresses that support the wall.

Throughout St Francis Church can be found plenty of extravagant gilding, some lovely wood carvings and beautiful hand painted tiles depicting biblical scenes in Portugal's traditional white and blue ceramic colouring, as well as some lovely frescos by famous Flemish artists.

Castle Walls

There has been a town on the site of Évora, Portugal, since Roman times thanks to its suitability as a strategic military point, raised high above the plains of the Alentejo and presiding over the area.

The old citadel, or acropolis, was built around the highest point in keeping with tradition. Over the course of centuries, defensive barriers Castle Walls were erected in order to protect the town, in turn elevating it to yet further prominence as a cultural, military and ecclesiastic centre of renown.

The initial construction of the Castle Walls was carried out by the Romans, with the Moors making later repairs and improvements, though little remains today of these original sections. Known as the Cerca Velha in Portuguese, these walls are literally known locally as the "old circle".

With the expansion of the city, new walls were built to a larger footprint during the 1300s to increase the size of the area held within its limits. These walls were built to a grander design as well as a grander scale, encompassing forty reinforced towers and ten gates. One of the gates, the Porta de Alconchel, remains beautifully intact to the present day and faces the main road out of Évora that leads to Portugal's capital, Lisbon. Another, the Arch of D. Isabel, can be seen near the post office, leading onto Rua Dona Isabel. The latter is classified as a National Monument.

The Cerca Velha was further extended and reinforced during the seventeenth century under the orders of King Joao IV after Portugal declared its independence from Spain. King Joao IV rightly sensed the possibility of an attack from the Spanish, which came in 1663, and the extensive walls were almost certainly to thank for Portugal's ability to fight off the attack and retain power.

Perhaps unsurprisingly, it is these later sections that remain most intact to the present day and are most prominent as you make your way through the streets of Lisbon. Take the time to pop into the

Ministry of Culture during your visit to Évora and ask for some more detailed information about the Castle Walls. They are well-informed and happy to tell you the best route to take to explore them in their entirety, including taking in some local Roman houses displaying centuries-old frescoes inside.

Évora Cathedral

Évora Cathedral is located right in the heart of the Old Town, close to many of the city's most famous ecclesiastical buildings. Known in Portugal as the Sé Catedral de Évora, it is an attractive mix of Romanesque and Gothic architecture and its ancient sections date from AD1200. It is one of the most visited monuments in the city, making part of the area of Évora that has been designated a UNESCO World Heritage site for its architectural and historical significance.

The imposing façade faces out onto the main square and overlooks the city spires and rooftops, located as it is at the highest point in Évora. It is constructed mainly in rose granite and is reminiscent of Lisbon Cathedral, with its two huge towers (added in the sixteenth century) and entrance gallery. The original gothic features include a huge window with a period tracery that provides most of the light to the interior. The two towers boast different spires and decoration and are both equally attractive in their own right.

Évora Cathedral's main portal is a beautiful example of Portugal's gothic sculpture tradition and the attractive marble columns are decorated with enormous statues of the Apostles. The design is similar to that of Notre Dame and Chartres Cathedrals in France and it is without doubt the most impressive example of its kind in Portugal. Historians believe these date back to the mid-fourteenth century and were possibly sculpted by renowned sculptors of the time, Mestre Pero and Telo Garcia.

Évora Cathedral is equally impressive inside as it is out. The interior is formed into a nave with two aisles, with a centrepiece of an eighteenth-century altar that is a study in period opulence, in pink, black and white marble. This section was created by the German architect Friedrich Ludwig, as was the choir.

The fifteenth-century sculpture of a pregnant Virgin Mary is unusual for its obvious display of her swollen stomach and is something of a pilgrimage site for young women from the local area who come here to pray for their fertility, or for partners and family members of pregnant women to pray for an easy labour and childbirth.

The Gothic cloister leads to an open terrace and some lovely views out over the surrounding Alentejo countryside. The Sé Catedral de Évora houses the Museum of Sacred Art in its south tower with some interesting pieces of religious art and over a thousand precious stones.

Praça Do Giraldo

Évora, Portugal, offers one of the most attractive and complete Old Town settings in mainland Europe. Designated a UNESCO World Heritage site for its architectural and historical significance, the old walled citadel of Évora remains to this day at the very heart of the city, both culturally and geographically.

The spacious Praça do Giraldo, or Giraldo Square, is flanked on four sides by some of the most impressive examples of gothic and Romanesque architecture on the Iberian Peninsula, a collection of ecclesiastical buildings and ancient palaces, clustered around the lovely pedestrianised cobbled central area and fountain. Giraldo Square is a place where locals congregate by day and by night to chat, drink coffee (or something a little stronger) and watch the world go by.

It is unsurprisingly a favourite starting point for tourists arriving in Évora during their trip to Portugal to visit the wonderful buildings and drink in this magical city's sense of history.

The Praça do Giraldo is bursting with life at all times of day. These days many of the white and ochre buildings have been converted into boutique pousadas and bed and breakfast hotels, perfect for visitors who want to stay right in the heart of the action. But it is the buildings such as the Sa Cathedral, the Temple of Diana that really dominate proceedings.

Built in the second Century by the Romans, no-one is quite sure how the Temple of Diana earned its name, but it is certainly worth a visit. It was one of Portugal's most important military outposts for many years following the town's heyday as the headquarters of the Roman military commander Quintus Sertorius. It offers beautiful views up to the prominent gothic and Romanesque cathedral that oversees the city.

As the story goes, the explorer Vasco de Gama had the flags of his ships blessed at the cathedral before he set sail from Portugal on his ground breaking voyage to India. The cathedral now houses a museum with interesting historical information and artifacts including a rare thirteenth-century ivory statue of the Virgin Mary.

Located in the heart of Giraldo Square is St. Anton's Church, the Igreja de Santo Antão which showcases some beautiful architecture dating back to the sixteenth Century.

The Praça do Giraldo was once used as an execution ground during the times of the Spanish Inquisition and makes for an interesting, if rather gruesome, place to start your tour of Évora.

Where to Eat

Best Restaurants in Évora

Restaurants in Évora, Portugal, vary from the strictly traditional to gastronomic five-star dining. This UNESCO World Heritage city is full of cobbled streets and sixteenth-century buildings just begging to be discovered, and hidden behind the old stone walls of white and ochre are myriad options for tasting the best of the local food and wine.

The <u>restaurants in Évora</u> can be more or less classified into three types: small and friendly, something special, and strictly traditional.

The vaulted ceilings of the <u>Taverna Restaurant</u> give a feeling of space to what is actually a small and cosy dining room, with wooden tables and chairs packed in closely together, conducive to fun and conversation both with your own party and fellow diners. This is a family-run affair offering delicious food prepared with local ingredients freshly shipped in from the nearby farms of the Alentejo.

Another family-run favourite is the <u>Tasquinha do Oliveira</u>, one of the quirkiest eateries in Évora. This is more like being invited to a dinner party at the home of a good friend than eating out in a restaurant. The tiny dining room has just five tables seating a total of twelve diners and is decorated in the traditional style of regional Portugal.

For a special meal, head to <u>O Fialho Restaurant</u>. This establishment is something of an institution within this historic city, dating back to 1948 and offering a delicious fusion of modern European and traditional flavours brought together with care and flair by a highly talented chef. You will feel this one in the pocket but it is well worth the extra spend.

<u>Divinus Restaurant</u> is another excellent choice for a special or celebratory meal. It is located in one of the city's most famous historic buildings, the restored fifteenth-century <u>Convento do Espinheiro</u>, which is now a five-star luxury hotel. This makes for one of the most unique and attractive dining options you could enjoy during

your trip to Portugal and is well worth a visit if you have a hankering for some fine food and wine.

Located in the heart of the historic centre in the building of the sixteenth-century Sepulveda Palace, Degust'AR is Évora's ultimate in sophistication. Low, white vaulted ceilings dominate the proceedings, and yet the sixteenth-century architecture is offset beautifully by a contemporary feel and wonderful twenty-first-century décor.

Almedina Restaurant is the type of institution that is kind on the wallet whilst providing a real education on the local cuisine. The food here is traditional, featuring many dishes that are particular to the Alentejo region. The daily chef's specials are well worth a try and the a la carte options are plentiful and varied.

Another traditional favourite, located off a small side street, is the <u>Luar de Janeiro</u> restaurant. It has a long reputation as a provider of some of the best regional cookery in the town and has been rewarded for its efforts with several accolades and prizes.

There is so much to choose from in Évora food and wine, do take more than a day or two to discover the best that this historic city has to offer

Divinus Restaurant

Divinus Restaurant in Évora is located in one of the city's most famous historic buildings, the fifteenth-century Convento do Espinheiro, which has been carefully restored and transformed into a five-star luxury hotel.

This restaurant in Évora makes for one of the most unique and attractive dining options you could enjoy during your trip to Portugal and is well worth a visit if you find yourself in this UNESCO World Heritage city.

Divinus Restaurant will take you on a gastronomic tour of the tastes of Portugal's Alentejo. Yet unlike many restaurants in Évora, it does not stick to rustic versions of the area's most famous dishes, it meshes them beautifully with the best of Mediterranean cooking to create a delightful fusion of regional and international flavours.

The dining room itself is found in the former wine cellar of the Convent's monks, a huge room with tall, vaulted light stone ceilings set off to perfection with crisp white linen and deep red upholstered chairs that are so comfortable that the delicious food is not the only reason you will not want your meal to end.

Divinus Restaurant makes for a more formal dining experience than many of the other restaurants in town. The front of house team is as well trained as you would expect of five-star hotel staff and the sommelier is knowledgeable and happy to share his wisdom about the contents of the restaurant's modern-day wine cellar.

Chef Luis Mourão has been in residence since December 2009 and has gained extensively through his training and participation in gastronomic events all over the world, from Germany to Brazil, before arriving to take his place at the forefront of Évora's gastronomic scene. His ethos is to make even the simplest foods a study in perfection and to embrace the best of the Alentejo, and by and large he is deemed to have succeeded.

One of the most popular ways to eat at Divinus Restaurant is to choose a selection of the "petiscos" or starters and eat them tapas style.

This enables you to taste multiple dishes and share them with your dining partners, to really give you an idea of the unique twist on local Alentejo flavours that the chef has created here. A "tapas" suggestion menu is available at €17.50, with the dishes especially selected by the chef each day. Dishes such as "Estremoz", a roasted traditional sausage, hot breaded goats cheese with tomato jam and oregano, mini octopus, sautéed clams and grilled lobster are guaranteed to tantalise the taste buds.

All in all an excellent restaurant in Évora and well worth a visit.

Divinus Restaurant
Convento do Espinheiro, Hotel & Spa
7002-502 Évora
Portugal
Tel: +351 266 788 200
Email: reservations@conventodoespinheiro.com

Almedina Restaurant

The Almedina Restaurant in Évora is located in the heart of the old town, amongst the cobbled streets and period buildings that characterise this popular UNESCO World Heritage city.

The building in which Almedina Restaurant is located is something of a historical destination in its own right, dating back over 500 years and offering a dining room full of traditional local character. The imposing ceiling of vaulted arches is made entirely of local marble and the embossed cross that is set within the stonework is a reminder of the building's origins as the property of Évora's Church.

The dining room is larger than it looks, too, with its relatively unassuming frontage opening out inside into a sweeping L-shaped room that is full of diners at both lunch and dinner sittings.

This is the type of restaurant in Évora that is kind on the wallet whilst providing a real education on the local cuisine. The food here is traditional, featuring many dishes that are particular to the Alentejo region. The daily chef's specials are well worth a try and the a la carte options are plentiful and varied. The Bacalhau (traditional salt cod, which is very popular in Portugal) is excellent opt for the Bacalhau Divino to taste it at its best. Roasted lamb stew is another favourite, the Sea bass is delicious and the Migas Alentejanas, a type of fried corn bread mixed up with tender pork and orange, comes highly recommended.

Service is excellent at Évora's Almedina Restaurant, with the front of house staff giving their visitors a warm welcome, eager to please with suggestions from the menu. Ask for recommendations from the wine list to match your meal and they will be happy to help though it is hard to go wrong if you order any local wine from the Alentejo region, this being one of Portugal's leading areas for wine production.

The owners themselves take great pleasure in chatting with their customers and sharing their stories and wisdom both about the local area and the delicious cuisine from this region of Portugal.

This is a good honest restaurant serving well-cooked, unpretentious dishes and well worth a visit while you are in Évora. It is also kind to the budget with a three-course a la carte meal costing as little as fifteen euros per head.

Almedina Restaurant
7000-553 Évora, Portugal
Tel: +351 969 405 415 or +351 967 462 010
Email: Almedina-Restaurante@hotmail.com

Bl Lounge Restaurant

The BL Lounge Restaurant in Évora is something of a departure for Évora eateries. Located right in the heart of the historic Old Town, next to the famous temple of Diana in Rua das Alcaçarias, this excellent restaurant offers modern fusion cuisine in a contemporary and well-designed dining room.

The traditional architectural exterior gives no clue as to the sophisticated and airy dining room that is hidden behind its walls. So many of the restaurants in Évora are in Portugal's Old World style and whilst that is somehow fitting of the city's ancient setting, it is also refreshing to find something that bucks the trend.

The BL Lounge Restaurant is set in a large dining room, tastefully decorated in whites with flourishes of purple and silver and with its well-stocked wine cellar prominently on show down the length of one of the side walls. The tables are spacious and the chairs comfortable.

The modern fusion cuisine also makes a pleasant change from the traditional flavours of Portugal's Alentejo region, which feature heavily on most of the menus in town. BL Lounge Restaurant draws on influences from all over Portugal and further afield to add a unique twist to its gastronomic offerings and its efforts have been rewarded recently with its first ever listing in the famed Michelin Guide, the 'bible' of worldwide cuisine.

Antonio, the owner, ensures his team offer a warm welcome and that guests are well looked after during their meal. He is very knowledgeable about the local Alentejo wines and happy to suggest the best bottle to suit your meal. Menu highlights include beautifully tender octopus or oven-baked cheese with oregano and raspberry jelly for starters, whilst tasty mains include risotto with asparagus and shrimp or roast beef in red wine with tomato migas. There is plenty to choose from on the dessert trolley and don't be surprised if Antonio throws in a complimentary glass of his famous grappa or house distilled brandy.

There is a separate lounge area, which is the perfect place to retreat for a coffee or liqueur after your meal and is a popular bar area in its own right amongst Évora's residents and many visitors.

BL Lounge Restaurant
Rua das Alcaçarias nº 1
7000-587 Évora, Portugal
Tel: +351 266 771 323
blounge@iol.pt

Degust'ar Restaurant

The Degust'AR Restaurant in Évora is one of the most luxurious and glamorous in this historic city of central Portugal. Located in the heart of the historic centre in the building of the sixteenth-century Sepulveda Palace, it retains many of the original architectural features for which this UNESCO World Heritage city has earned its fame.

The décor is perhaps the best of any restaurant in Évora. Low, white vaulted ceilings dominate the proceedings, and yet the sixteenth-century architecture is offset beautifully by a contemporary feel and wonderful twenty-first-century décor. The use of light woods, plenty of glass, crisp white linen and splashes of muted colours has created a dining room which feels spacious, airy and more than a little bit special.

Couple this with the outdoor terrace area for al fresco eating under the stars in Portugal's balmy summer evenings and it is easy to see why this restaurant in Évora has gained such popularity.

Degust'AR Restaurant was the brainchild of award-winning chef Antonio Nobre. Nobre is more than just a chef, he is something of a national name, having published several well-known recipe books and made regular appearances on Portugal's TV stations presenting and guest featuring on cookery programmes. His cookery embraces the aromatic flavours of the Alentejo with its pig rearing and olive growing traditions, bringing a modern European twist to centuries-old recipes.

Start your meal with the tasty "couvert" for two to get the gastronomic juices flowing. Follow up with game smoked sausage sautéed with turnip leaves and quails eggs or crunchy Serpa cheese with sun-dried fruits and wild rocket salad. Tasty mains include octopus sautéed in garlic olive oil with potato porridge and tomato, green beans and regional crunchy bread or traditional Évora favourites with a modern twist such as Alentejo dogfish soup, or pork kidneys in wine.

The wine cellar takes pride of place along one of the restaurant's main walls, with hundreds of bottles on show within their especially created glassed-in storage display. The list features a plethora of offerings from all over Portugal, including of course a large selection of the local Alentejo offerings.

Ask the sommelier to select a suitable bottle to match your food order, or opt for the tasting menu which comes with a selection of wines pre-selected to perfectly set off the delights of your meal at Degust'AR Restaurant.

Degust'AR Restaurant
Rua Cândido dos Reis 72
7000-782 Évora, Portugal
Tel: +351 266 740 700
Fax: +351 266 740 735.
Email: geral@mardearhotels

O Fialho Restaurant

O Fialho Restaurant in Évora, Portugal, is something of an institution within this historic city. Founded as far back as 1948 by Manuel Fialho as a chophouse, it has evolved and grown through the decades to become possibly the most famous restaurant in Évora.

Évora is set within the Ribatejo region of Portugal and O Fialho Restaurant has specialized since its inception in embracing the traditional dishes and tastes of the region. During the 1960s it became a "casa de pasto", serving government officials and other members of public office when they were in Évora, and the building underwent some renovation and remodeling works with the help of a well-known local architect.

Throughout the years, Manuel's three children Amor, Gabriel and Manuel worked with their father as the restaurant built its client base and reputation and these days it is the award-winning chef Gabriel who excels in the kitchen and carries on the name his father established more than 60 years ago.

After a brief spell of focusing heavily on modern European cooking, O Fialho Restaurant soon returned to its traditional Alentejo roots and it is this focus that it has retained ever since.

The dining room is large and welcoming and the staff friendly and helpful. This is an upscale restaurant but that certainly does not mean the staff is pompous or the setting intimidating. Choose from mouth-watering dishes such as Wild Asparagus with egg or Quail eggs with local "paio" a rustic sausage typical of this area of Portugal.

The most famous dish must be the Wild boar tenderloins with apple do try to ensure someone in your party orders it so you can all have a taste!

Other great options are the Convento da Cartuxa Partridge or Oven-baked lamb, all followed up with delicious homemade desserts in typical style.

This is the kind of restaurant you may only visit once or twice during your stay in Portugal thanks to its higher than average prices but it is well worth a visit for a budget-blowing meal of extravagance.

O Fialho? Restaurant
7000-557 Évora, Portugal
Tel: +351 266 70 30 79
Fax: +351 266 74 48 73

Tasquinha Do Oliveira

Tasquinha do Oliveira Restaurant in Évora is considered to be one of the quirkiest eateries in this historic UNESCO World Heritage city of central Portugal.

Run by the husband and wife team of Manuel, who manages the front of house, and Carolina who creates the dishes behind the scenes in the kitchen, it is more like spending an evening in the dining room at a friend's house than eating out in a restaurant in Évora. Just five tables seating a total of 14 guests are squeezed into the tiny dining room, which is delightfully decorated in the true styles of regional Portugal.

The whitewashed walls play host to framed pictures and many accolades won by the Tasquinha do Oliveira for its contribution to gastronomy in the city.

When you arrive you are greeted by Manuel, who will show you to your table ready laid and set out with a selection of five or six tasty looking starters. Do be aware that, like many restaurants in Portugal, these dishes are charged for if they are eaten but if they do not all appeal then you have a right to (and indeed are expected to) ask for them to be removed back to the kitchen. Many visitors find themselves caught by this during their stay in Évora simply by not knowing the local dining etiquette.

Manuel is happy to make suggestions for main courses or let you take your pick from the dishes on the menu. The partridge dishes are excellent thanks to the strong tradition of game rearing in the Évora area and the black pork and clams is a classic. Monkfish and rice is another popular favourite and there is plenty for diners to choose from to suit every palette.

When you arrive you are greeted by Manuel, who will show you to your table ready laid and set out with a selection of five or six tasty looking starters. Do be aware that, like many restaurants in

Portugal, these dishes are charged for if they are eaten but if they do not all appeal then you have a right to (and indeed are expected to) ask for them to be removed back to the kitchen. Many visitors find themselves caught by this during their stay in Évora simply by not knowing the local dining etiquette.

Manuel is happy to make suggestions for main courses or let you take your pick from the dishes on the menu. The partridge dishes are excellent thanks to the strong tradition of game rearing in the Évora area and the black pork and clams is a classic. Monkfish and rice is another popular favourite and there is plenty for diners to choose from to suit every palette.

experience.

If you want to experience the delights of Alentejo cooking in a pretty environment that has the welcoming cosiness of a friend's home, the Tasquinha do Oliveira is an excellent choice.

Tasquinha do Oliveira Restaurant
Rua Cândido dos Reis 45
7000-582 São Mamede
Évora, Portugal
Tel: +351 266 744 841
Fax: +351 266 752 905
Email: tasquinha.oliveira@gmail.com

Reckless

Luar De Janeiro

Located off a small side street in the historic town of Évora, Portugal is one of the best eateries in the area. Luar de Janeiro restaurant has a long reputation as a provider of some of the best regional cookery in the town and has been rewarded for its efforts with several accolades and prizes.

This is the ideal restaurant in Évora to sample the traditional delicacies of the Alentejo. Here you will find them cooked to perfection and served by friendly, welcoming and knowledgeable staff, which makes a great effort to ensure their guests enjoy not just the delicious food but also their whole dining experience.

The entrance is off a small cobbled road but opens out into a lovely dining room, which although decorated in traditional style with whitewashed walls and dark carved wooden furniture, is somewhat more sophisticated and elegant than other restaurants of its type in Évora. The Luar de Janeiro Restaurant dates back several decades and began life as a "tasquinha", a kind of snack bar and tavern that is popular in Portugal.

Originally specialising in poultry dishes and snacks such as tasty garlic-infused snails, it moved on to expand its menu to include many of the regional favourites of this Alentejo region in Portugal.

These days Luar de Janeiro Restaurant in Évora is a byword for gastronomy.

The best way to eat here is to order a selection of small starters from the menu as soon as you arrive, to give you time to savour the delicious flavours of the local cheeses, asparagus, cold meats and so on. The restaurant still specialises in poultry and game, offering some delicious partridge and duck dishes on its extensive list of main courses. The baked goat is also delicious, literally falling off the bone and tastes superb washed down with a glass of the local Alentejo wine.

The wine list is particularly well-chosen, featuring not just local bottles (though it is hard to go wrong if you choose one of these) but also a good selection of vintages and grapes from all over the country and beyond.

Prices are higher than many establishments in Évora, but then so is the quality to match. So if you decide to push the boat out one evening during your stay in order to sample some of the best food this historic city has to offer, Luar de Janeiro Restaurant is the place to do so

Luar de Janeiro
Travessa do Janeiro, 13
7000-600 Évora, Portugal
Tel: +351 266 749 114 /5
Fax: +351 266 749 116
Email: restaurante@luardejaneiro.com

Taverna Restaurant

When you go in search of a good restaurant in Évora, Travessa de Santa Marta is probably the best place to start. This delightful cobbled street in the heart of the Old Town is full to bursting with eateries serving the rustic, traditional cuisine of the Alentejo region of Portugal. Much of the street is taken up with the whitewashed buildings dating back some 500 years to times when the Church was in its heyday in Évora, and formerly belonged to the convent of Santa Marta.

The vaulted ceilings of the restaurant give a feeling of space to what is actually a small and cosy dining room, with wooden tables and chairs packed in closely together, conducive to fun and conversation both with your own party and fellow diners. Taverna Restaurant is owned by Luis and Rosario Dias, with Luis running the show front of house and Rosario behind the scenes in the kitchen, preparing mouth-watering dishes with fresh farm ingredients from rural Portugal.

Luis is a jovial character, happy to chat and make friends with his customers. Do take the time to ask him for recommendations not just from the food menu but also from the wine list which features a number of tasty Alentejo wines.

With main courses ranging from seven to ten euros, Taverna restaurant is a good option for well-cooked local food without a hefty price tag.

Start with chickpeas and salt cod, one of Portugal's specialities, or opt for local olives, wild mushrooms or Paio, the delicious rustic sausage that is very popular in Évora and the local area. Pork features heavily in Alentejo cuisine and is well represented on the menu here.

Try the slow-roasted pork spare ribs that literally fall off the bone, or the migas, the traditional dish made from fried and mashed corn bread with seasoned pork and chunks of orange. Lots of custard-based traditional desserts provide an excellent option to finish your meal.

One of the biggest draws of Taverna Restaurant in Évora, however, is its set-price fixed menu of the day. For just €5.75 (prices are correct at time of writing but do check on arrival) guests can enjoy a three-course set meal with a complimentary drink.

The set menu usually features a bowl of home-made soup with bread, veal or pork for main and fruit or ice cream for dessert, all washed down with a complimentary glass of liqueur or a soft drink.

This may not be Michelin-starred gastronomy, but Taverna Restaurant is sure to leave you with a lovely taste of Évora at its best.

Taverna Restaurant
Travessa de Santa Marta 5
7000-553 Évora, Portugal
Tel: +351 266 700 747
Email: geral@restaurantetaverna.com

Best Things to Do in Évora

Évora, Portugal, lies in the southern centre of the area, some 130km east of Lisbon in the heart of the Alentejo region. Set amongst the rolling hills and expansive plains swathed in vines, it makes the perfect base from which to explore all that this famous wine-producing area has to offer.

It is also an important tourist destination in its own right thanks to its long history and modern-day designation as a UNESCO World Heritage site. As a result there are many things to do in Évora and plenty of exploring to be done right on your doorstep.

Whether you travel to Évora, Portugal for its historic monuments, regional gastronomy, musical events or lively student-led nightlife, there are plenty of things to do in Évora to keep you occupied from dawn until dusk.

Gastronomy delights

The Alentejo region is famed for its delicious cuisine and there are plenty of restaurants in Évora in which to sample it. There is a strong pig-rearing tradition in the local area, ensuring that tender, succulent pork features strongly on every menu, along with tasty Serpa cheese, plenty of hearty lamb and offal dishes and of course a good dose of mouth-watering sweet treats.

Restaurants in Évora embrace the best that the region has to offer in a range of settings, from fine dining to rustic and romantic.

Day and night

Nightlife in Évora is largely led by its student population, thanks to its position as one of Portugal's leading university towns. Nightlife in Évora is relaxed and fun-packed, with plenty of bars in which to enjoy a relaxed glass of the local nectar and enough late-night dancing clubs to keep die-hard dancing fans on their toes.

Most of the action is centred in the narrow streets of the old town, behind the walls of the many sixteenth-century whitewashed and ochre façades.

The annual calendar is bursting with events in Évora to be celebrated at all times of the year. From New Year fireworks and revelry and colourful mardi gras to the summer music festivals that embrace both the classical and modern genres, whenever you travel to Évora, Portugal, you are assured of a warm welcome and plenty to celebrate

Cultural Tour

The UNESCO World Heritage city of Évora is often referred to as a "cidade-museu" or "museum city" and it is easy to understand why. Walking through the winding streets of its ancient-walled old town is like walking through a museum in itself, a journey through thousands of years of architectural, military and cultural history as you make your way past the St Francis Church with its eerie Chapel of Bones, Évora Cathedral, the ancient Roman Temple of Diana and the imposing sixteenth-century viaduct, one of the most impressive feats of engineering of its time.

However, there are many cultural attractions besides, from old-school museums such as the Museu de Évora, or Évora Museum, to modern art spaces such as the Fundação Eugenio de Almeida.

Évora Museum

Start your discovery of Évora's cultural attractions at the Évora Museum. First established in 1915, it is located within the old Paço Episcopal, though its history stretches back still further. In 1804 the Archbishop of Évora, Friar Manuel do Cenaculo, inaugurated a public library, which also formed part of his art, archaeological and natural collections. It was transferred to the state in 1839, but it was not until after the declaration of Independence that it opened formally as a public museum.

As the collection expanded, so the need to find a larger home for it grew and plans were made for it to move to the Palacio Amaral. When the Palacio Amaral was seriously damaged in 1926, it was finally installed in the Bishop's Palace, opening once again in 1929 in its new and permanent home.

The Évora Museum showcases around 20,000 pieces, including paintings, sculptures, and archaeological artifacts dating back to Roman and Gothic times and the period of the Moorish occupation. The pieces serve to tell the story of Portugal, and Évora itself, through the ages, from early days to the height of the empire and beyond.

The exhibition as a whole is thoughtfully organised in a way that brings together various fields of knowledge as well as periods in History, to great effect.

The avant-garde Fundação Eugenio de Almeida is a modern exhibition space close to Évora Cathedral.

The Fundação Eugenio de Almeida plays host to ad hoc exhibitions by local artists, national artists of standing and the occasional big-name international such as Marcel Duchamp.

Évora Cathedral

Most visitors to Évora will take the time to explore its imposing cathedral. Évora Cathedral is a majestic building that sits at the highest point of the city, presiding over the old walled citadel since it was built at the end of the fifteenth century.

The grand façade of rose granite is offset dramatically by the two large towers that sit either side. It is in the South Tower that the Museum of Sacred Art is located.

The Museum of Sacred Art is well worth a visit for anyone with an interest in ecclesiastical art and history. It is home to a wide collection of religious art and a large number of precious stones, numbering in excess of a thousand.

From Évora Cathedral, make your way on to the Palacio Cadaval for an interesting mix of ecclesiastical art and antiques from old world Portugal. The Palacio Cadaval also provides an interesting window onto daily life in a bygone age and is home to a 600-square-metre collection of exquisitely crafted eighteen-century "azulejos", or traditional tiles.

For a little light relief from ancient history and artifacts, complete your cultural tour of Évora with a trip to the Aldeia da Terra. The Aldeia da Terra was the brainchild of two local sculptors, Tiago Cabeça and Magda Ventura. These two remarkable artists bring together the ancient Portuguese traditions of hand-painted ceramics with a delightfully modern and humours edge.

Aldeia Da Terra

The Aldeia da Terra takes the form of an entire miniature village, mirroring the old town of Évora. It comes complete with miniature monuments, whitewashed and ochre sixteenth-century houses and modern-day cars, taxis, bicycles.

The finishing flourish comes in the form of the ceramic figures going about their day-to-day lives, paying homage to the past and present of this delightful Portuguese city.

Festivals & Events

As a student city, Évora may have an ancient exterior but culturally it is certainly young at heart.

There is much in Évora to entertain the masses every week of the year, from regular cultural events to major spectaculars that take place throughout the streets and ancient buildings of this picturesque UNESCO World Heritage city.

New Year Celebrations

Portugal is renowned for its New Year celebrations and Évora is no exception. Shortly before midnight the town's streets flood with people to ring in the New Year to the accompaniment of fireworks, music and dancing. As with most countries in Europe, January 1st is a public holiday in Portugal.

Carnival or Mardi Gras comes next, usually in early March. Mardi Gras is celebrated all over Portugal with a week of colourful street parties aimed at the young and the old alike. Colourful floats, firecrackers, fireworks, fancy dress parades, musical concerts and a whole army of colourful decorations are sure to entertain.

Holy Week falls during the week before Easter and is celebrated all over Portugal thanks to the country's strong Roman Catholic tradition. Colourful processions and fill the streets of Évora making Holy Week a lively and interesting time to visit.

Both Freedom Day and Labour Day are major public holidays in Portugal so it is worth being aware of bank and shop closures and of course the entertainments that go with them. Freedom Day falls on April 25th each year while Labour Day falls on May 1st.

Summer Is Here

June marks the beginning of the busy summer season in Évora. The highlight of early summer is without a doubt the Feira São João, or St John's

Fair, which has been celebrated in Portugal for more than six centuries.

The Feira São João in Évora is one of the largest in the country and certainly the most popular in the Alentejo region.

The event lasts for no less than 12 days and is marked by craft fairs, gastronomy and music in the streets as well as a number of scheduled cultural activities in various locations throughout the town. Expect to see pavement barbecues, Fado and other bands and impromptu dancing in the streets, along with plenty of traditional costumes and a good dose of fireworks.

The Évora Classical Music Festival, or Festival Évora Classica, has grown from a small-scale three-day event to become one of Europe's leading classical music festivals in the annual calendar. These days the Évora Classical Music Festival brings together some of the world's leading orchestras and performers at the town's cultural centrepiece of the Palacio de Cadaval. Each year the festival showcases a particular genre of classical music from a particular part of the world, including in past years such spectacles as Rajasthani dancers and Hungarian gypsy fiddlers.

Following the musical theme, the end of July sees the Festival Alentejo. The Festival Alentejo is a modern music festival, which takes place over a three-day period and features some major household music names from the past and present. Rock, pop and dance music vie for position on the many stages and the festival draws a large audience from all over Portugal and beyond.

As the summer draws to a close, so does the festival season but there is still plenty to see and do in Évora to keep visitors entertained 365 days per year. Évora is a student city, home to the oldest University in the country, so there is never any shortage of a party.

If you are in Évora in the autumn, don't miss All Souls' Day on November 1st. All Souls' Day is celebrated all over Portugal and indeed in many parts of the world, to remember those who have passed away.

Shortly afterwards comes FIKE, the Évora International Short Film Festival. Whether you are a cinematography aficionado or simply enjoy watching a good film, the Évora International Short Film Festival is a delight. Scores of short films are screened during the festival, created by some of the most exciting up and coming filmmakers from all over the world.

Restoration of Independence Day is the last major holiday before Christmas arrives and the year draws to a close. Restoration of Independence Day falls on December 1st. And finally Christmas in Évora is a colourful occasion and a popular time for family get-togethers and public celebrations. Christmas is usually marked on the evening of 24th December, leaving 25th for contemplation, relaxation and perhaps sleeping off the excesses of the day before

History at Its Best

The UNESCO World Heritage city of Évora offers many attractions for visitors to enjoy. There is plenty to keep visitors entertained for several days in the city, however if you in Évora for just one day there is a surprising amount that you can see and do.

As Évora has evolved and grown from a small, walled town first established in Roman times, its primary attractions have remained centrally located, clustered mostly in and around the ancient citadel that occupies its highest point, presiding over the maze of winding streets and historic buildings below.

Walking through the streets of Évora is like taking a walk through history. The town is something of a living, breathing museum celebrating Portugal's rich and diverse history of conflicts and conquests, exploration and independence.

Praça Do Giraldo

The lively Praça do Giraldo is the perfect place to start any tour of Évora. The square is flanked on all four sides by a series of historic buildings dating back several centuries, and in some cases more than 2000 years. Here you will come across some of the most impressive examples of Gothic and Romanesque architecture to be found anywhere on the Iberian Peninsula, a collection of ecclesiastical buildings and ancient palaces, clustered around the lovely pedestrianised cobbled central area and fountain.

The Praça do Giraldo is the perfect place to relax over a drink or bite to eat at one of its many cafes and bars. If you are staying in self-catering accommodations or if your hotel does not include breakfast, start your sightseeing day here with a leisurely breakfast in the sun at one of the outdoor tables of the pavement cafes. There is nothing quite like the strong aroma of freshly brewed Brazilian coffee beans and a Portuguese "pastel de nata" (a type of mouth-wateringly delicate custard tart) to get your day of historical explorations off to a flying start.

Temple of Diana

The ruins of the Roman Temple of Diana are located on one edge of the square, dating back some 2000 years to the days when Évora was one of Portugal's most important Roman military outposts. Diana was the goddess of the moon, the hunt and chastity in ancient Rome and the temple was dedicated to her upon its construction in 100AD.

Historians believe that there would have been other similar temples built in the city around the same era, however if this is the case there is little surviving evidence of them now. The Temple of Diana is exceptionally strong, no doubt the reason for its survival as the devastating earthquake of 1755 razed many similar buildings to the ground. The Temple of Diana has had many uses throughout the ages, from execution site during the Inquisition to slaughterhouse in the nineteenth century.

Évora Cathedral

Heading up the square away from the Temple of Diana, you will reach Évora Cathedral, an attractive combination of Gothic and Romanesque architecture. Évora Cathedral is set at the very highest point of the old citadel, in a dominant position presiding over the winding streets of the city below. It boasts an impressive facia of rose granite, which is capped either side by two huge towers dating back to the sixteenth century.

Évora Cathedral is equally impressive inside as it is out. The ornate interior is a study in period opulence, boasting detailed frescoes, impressive sculptures and plenty of pink, black and white marble and stonework. Take a walk through the Gothic cloister to the open terrace to enjoy the sweeping views out across the Alentejo countryside before finishing up in the cathedral's Museum of Sacred Art in the south tower.

Chapel of Bones

Still in the heart of the UNESCO World Heritage site that covers much of the old town, you will arrive at St Francis Church and its famous Chapel of Bones. The St Francis Church is a fine example of late-fifteenth and early-sixteenth century architectural styles. However, its period architecture is not the only reason for visiting the church.

The Chapel of Bones was created by a group of Franciscan monks in an effort to free up some of the surrounding land, which was at the time taken up with no less than 42 different consecrated burial sites. Rather than bury the remains anew, the monks cemented them into the walls of the chapel as a reminder of their own mortality and a place for contemplation and prayer.

There are many other historic attractions to see and enjoy in Évora, many of which, such as the Agua de Prata Aqueduct and the castle walls can be admired simply by wandering through the winding streets of the old town. The Agua de Prata Aqueduct stretches for nine kilometres from its source right through the centre of town, and is one of Portugal's most impressive architectural works of the sixteenth century, while the old castle walls can be admired at every turn, the perfect reminder of Évora's rich, historic past

One Day Tour

There is much to keep visitors to Évora occupied for several days of sightseeing in and around the city. But if you are travelling by car or feel like hiring one for a day in order to venture a little further afield, there are some delightful day trips to the outlying areas just waiting to be discovered.

This one-day tour takes you away from UNESCO World Heritage sites of Évora to two very different Alentejo towns, each with their own distinct heritage and much to please the inquisitive traveller.

Begin your tour by heading due north from Évora, across the rolling hills and plains of prime wine-growing country. The land and climate here are perfectly suited to wine production, and indeed some of the very best wines produced in Portugal are produced here in the Alentejo. As a result, the broad plains that ease their way out from the historic city are swathed in vines, adding a distinctive flavour to the landscape.

Multicolour Weaving Tradition

Your destination for the first leg of your trip is Arraiolos, a small town some 25 kilometres north of Évora with a pretty town centre populated by beautiful and well-maintained whitewashed houses, several churches such as the Rococo Baroque Matriz and the sixteenth-century Misericordia and a surprising number of shops selling a wide variety of colourful artisan rugs.

It is this carpet-making tradition that has led Arraiolos to develop a reputation that is far larger than you would expect for a small provincial town with just 3,500 inhabitants. The tradition dates back to the times of the Moorish occupation of the Iberian Peninsula and is based on a unique method of weaving in which many strands of thick, multi-coloured wool are worked with oblique stitches onto a basic foundation of cotton, sacking or linen. The different designs are now used to define the period in which they were invented and vary from intricate designs to broad, sweeping patterns.

The Arraiolos rugs cover a vast range of sizes, from very small to large enough to fill a spacious room and can be used on the floor or hung for ornamental purposes. It is a delight simply to wonder through the whitewashed streets, punctuated with bursts of colour from the rug shops dotted here and there displaying their wares. The owners are on the whole very friendly and helpful and many speak English and other languages apart from Portuguese. The rugs are guaranteed with a certificate of authenticity and make a lovely memento to take home from your trip to Portugal.

Be sure to try the local sweet-savoury pastries, known as Toucinhos before you head on to your next stop. From Arraiolos, head due east towards the border where Portugal meets Spain close to Badajoz, through yet more rolling Alentejo plains. Stopping short of the border is your destination, the historic town of Estremoz.

Marble Streets

Estremoz is a major marble-producing town and is the world's second-largest marble exporter, offering a huge variety of stone in different colours, veins and styles. So readily available is this attractive material that the walls of the town are swathed in it, transforming it into a colourful and opulent museum of marble.

Wandering through the streets of Estremoz is like taking a trip through Portugal's historical past and there are many impressive monuments and museums that are well worth a visit while you are here. Start at the 13th-century Torre das Tres Coroas that towers over the town. Now carefully transformed into an elegant pousada, residents and guests alike are welcomed into the Torre das Tres Coroas' pretty courtyard and landscaped gardens to appreciate the stunning view out over the town and the vast plains of the Alentejo.

From here, move onto the Museu Municipal, or Municipal Museum. The Municipal Museum is home to a wonderful collection of ecclesiastical art, local pottery and clay figures. If time permits, the Museu Rural and the Palacio da Touca are both well worth a visit too. The Museu Rural has some wonderful local artifacts on show while the Palacio da Touca boasts an elegant collection of fine 17th century tiles.

Simply wandering through the streets of Estremoz is a delight. Stop and enjoy a coffee and cake at one of the town's many pavement cafes, admire the colourful stonework and watch the world go by before heading back to Évora at the end of a satisfying day of sightseeing

Gastronomy Tour

The historic city of Évora is located in the heart of the Alentejo region of south central Portugal. The city's rich history dates back several thousand years and it is thanks to its long and distinguished heritage, coupled with the wonderful climatic characteristics of the region, that it has earned itself such a strong reputation for gastronomy and wine production.

As a result, visitors to Évora are well-advised to make time to indulge as much in discovering the city's delicious food and wine as its rich architectural and cultural history.

Begin your exploration of Évora's gastronomy and wine with a hearty breakfast, either buffet style in your hotel with plenty of freshly baked breads and cakes, home made jams and local cold meats and cheeses, or at one of the delightful pavement cafes, with a freshly brewed coffee and a mouth watering pastry, before heading further afield to learn more about Évora's rich gastronomy and wine-producing history.

Exploring The Vineyards

The Alentejo is one of Portugal's leading wine producing regions, with kilometre after kilometre of gentle hills and expansive plains around Évora swathed in vineyards. Here, thanks to the unique climatic conditions, the vines produce grapes of outstanding quality, perfectly suited to the production of some of Portugal's best wines.

There are six major species of vine that are mostly, though not exclusively, dedicated to the production of the best Alentejo wines. These include the zesty Roupeira, the refreshing Rabo de

Ovelha and the rich Antão Vaz, which are used in the production of the region's leading whites. The reds are mostly produced from the fruity Periquita, the rich Trincadeira and the full-bodied Aragonez.

Many of the local wineries offer guided tours, on which you will be taken around the estate to see how the vines grow, how the grapes are harvested, and learn about the production process. Tastings are of course a part of the trip, so choose your winery with care to ensure you taste the best of the best!

The Herdade do Esporão wine estate dates back more than 700 years to 1267 and still retains several of its historic buildings to this day, including the medieval tower and a chapel, both of which are protected national monuments. However, unlike some of the area's older wineries, the estate only turned to wine production in the early 1970s when the estate was bought by two young winemakers, Joaquim Bandeira and Dr Jose Alfredo Parreira Holtreman Roquette.

The young team have brought together the best of Old World winemaking knowledge with New World techniques which, combined with extensive investment, have catapulted it to fame as one of the most forward-thinking and successful wineries in the country, winning many accolades in the process.

One of the delights of a tour of the Herdade do Esporão wine estate is that the team have not just limited themselves to wine production, but have invested too in cultivating and producing high-end delicatessen products such as cheeses and olive oils, ensuring that your treat is a true treat for the taste buds.

A Heaven of Cheese

The Alentejo region is famous for its cheeses, smoked sausage and other cold meats, and all manner of pork products thanks to its long history of pig rearing. Take time to sample some of the regional specialities tapas-style for lunch. Serpa, Nisa and Évora cheeses are delicious with freshly baked bread as are soups such as gazpacho, river fish stew and "ensopado de borrego" (lamb stew soup). Fresh olives, dried fruits and local almonds also make tasty snacks to keep you going during a long day of sightseeing and if you feel the need for something sweet, try a "queijada", a traditional sweet cake made with cheese.

Back in the heart of Évora, splash out at least once during your stay for a high quality meal that brings together the best regional foods from this area of Portugal with gastronomic flair and a modern European twist. O Fialho Restaurant and

Degust'AR Restaurant are both able to offer quality of this type in abundance.

Award-Winning Delights

O Fialho Restaurant is something of an institution. Founded as far back as 1948 by Manuel Fialho as a chophouse, it has evolved and grown through the decades to become possibly the most famous restaurant in Évora.

Choose from mouth-watering dishes such as Wild Asparagus with egg or Quail eggs with local "paio" a rustic sausage typical of this area of Portugal. The most famous dish must be the Wild boar tenderloins with apple do try to ensure someone in your party orders it so you can all have a taste! Other great options are the Convento da Cartuxa Partridge or Oven-baked lamb, all followed up with delicious homemade desserts in typical style.

Degust'AR Restaurant was the brainchild of award-winning chef Antonio Nobre, a regular fixture on Portuguese TV cookery shows.

Indulge in game smoked sausage sautéed with turnip leaves and quails eggs or crunchy Serpa cheese with sun dried fruits and wild rocket salad. Tasty mains include octopus sautéed in garlic olive oil with potato porridge and tomato, green beans and regional crunchy bread or traditional Évora favourites with a modern twist such as Alentejo dogfish soup, or pork kidneys in wine.

Both restaurants boast a large and varied wine list with plenty of local Alentejo favourites to complete your gastronomic journey through the best of Évora food and wine

Nightlife in Évora

Évora, in Portugal, is an ancient city with a modern outlook. There is plenty here to keep visitors entertained from dawn to dusk and for those who are looking for some fun and lively Évora nightlife, entertainment from dusk until dawn shouldn't be any problem either.

Évora is a provincial town set around an hour's drive due east from Lisbon, located in south central Portugal. It is located in the Alentejo region, an area known for its wine production and some delicious traditional regional cookery, so as you might expect, eating and drinking play a major role in the lives of the town's inhabitants and the many visitors it receives each year.

Dinner Time

There are many restaurants and places to eat in Évora, including small cafés and bakeries, intimate restaurants offering excellent value set daily menus featuring the traditional cuisine of the region and five-star dining at some of the town's most exclusive boutique hotels. People in Portugal tend to eat later than they do in northern Europe or the States, and Évora is no exception. Don't expect to see many fellow diners keeping you company, other than fellow tourists, if you eat much before 9pm, and expect to see things in full swing at around 10pm.

One of the most popular places to congregate in the town is at the Praça do Giraldo, the central square right at the highest point of town, located in the old citadel within the ancient castle walls. The Praça do Giraldo is flanked on all four sides by some of the most famous buildings and monuments in this UNESCO World Heritage city and is as much of a meeting place at night as it is during the day.

The square is pedestrianized and lined with a series of pleasant cafés and other eateries, each of which offers outdoor tables where diners can sit and enjoy a drink or bite to eat throughout the warm, balmy Portuguese evenings, sharing conversation with friends and watching the world go by. Most establishments on the square stay open until around midnight, sometimes later in high season.

For a drink in an upmarket setting, try any one of the smart hotel bars, such as the Pousada de Évora, Convento dos Lóios or the Hotel M'AR de Aqueduto. The Hotel M'AR de Aqueduto offers one of the most attractive outdoor restaurant bars in the city, where you can enjoy fine food and drink against the backdrop of the floodlit aqueduct walls.

Évora is home to one of Portugal's leading universities and as a result it is very much a city that is young at heart. Student parties take places virtually every night of the week and the town's bars and lower-cost eateries are always buzzing with a lively crowd of bright young things.

Most of the bars are located within the historic centre and it is easy to make your way from one to the next without having to walk very far in between.

Wednesday night is student night in most of the bars and clubs and also in some of the town's restaurants. Expect to find larger crowds as a result but also a little extra atmosphere to go with them.

Dance The Night Away

For those in search of their dancing legs, head for Praxis Discoteca on the Rua Valdevinos. Praxis Discoteca is a dance club frequented by a mix of young locals and visitors on the sightseeing trail and is open from Monday to Saturday from 10pm to 6am. Entrance at the time of writing was 11 euros, which gives you access to four different bars, two different dance floors and two complimentary beers to get your evening started.

Café da Cidade is another popular hangout for locals and students, located on Rua das Alcaçarias. Open from 11am until 2am Café da Cidade is a lively bar, which transforms itself into a dance bar as the night warms up.

Évora is something of a living museum its architectural buildings and monuments date back to ancient times, with plenty of additions from the middle ages and the days of discovery. Wandering through the streets and simply drinking in the sights and sounds of the city is a delight not just during the day, but also at night.

The dramatic aqueduct and many sections of the castle walls are beautifully lit and make a wonderful backdrop for a night-time stroll through the cobbled streets. Some of the main sights are even open at night for visitors, such as the St Francis Church and its famous Chapel of Bones though entering this eerie site out of daylight hours is not for the faint hearted!

Shopping in Évora

As one of Portugal's older cities and a UNESCO World Heritage site, shopping does not tend to be at the top of the agenda for Évora's visitors. Nonetheless, there are some lovely shopping areas and plenty of traditional and modern retail finds to be had.

Whether you are looking for traditional pieces crafted from the local cork trees that grow in abundance, hand-painted ceramic tiles in traditional or modern style, jewellery, clothing and even furniture and accessories for the home, you are likely to find it somewhere in Évora.

Local Street Markets

A good way to start your discovery of Portugal's shopping is to explore the local markets. The municipal market offers plenty of colourful fresh produce, grown in the local area, where you can marvel at the reds, greens, yellows, purples and oranges on display. Be sure to stop at one of the stalls selling local artisan produce such as smoky "paio" pork sausage, Serpa cheese and fat, juicy olives. A few choice samples make the perfect lunchtime accompaniment for some freshly baked bread, consumed in the shade of the local Jardim Publico, or public park, right next door to the municipal market.

A vast open-air market takes place on the second Tuesday of each month at the Rossio de São Bras, just outside the old castle walls between the centre of town and the railway station. Here you will find all manner of handicrafts, household goods, traditional costumes, clothing, shoes, children's toys, accessories and just about everything else you can imagine. The quality varies, as with all open-air markets, but there are certainly some bargains to be had, especially if you get into the spirit of things and haggle.

Each weekend sees a rotation of four different markets at a spot close the Aqueduct. Depending on when you visit, you will find a focus on antiquities, old books, collectables, and arts and crafts. Be prepared to spend some time rooting through the wares on display and you are likely to find some real hidden gems.

Avenida 5 de Outubro is the main shopping street in Évora. Largely pedestrianized, it is located right in the heart of the old town close to the Praça do Giraldo with its imposing cathedral and Roman temple. Avenida 5 de Outubro makes a lovely place for a stroll amongst the old doorways that open out to a plethora of shops selling colourful pottery, hand-painted ceramic tiles, carved cork adornments and the usual range of t-shirts, postcards and souvenirs found in the tourist towns.

One of the most special places for shopping in Évora has to be the Oficina da Terra located on the Rua do Raimundo. This is a ceramics studio where two young local artists, Tiago Cabeça and Magda Ventura produce and hand paint exquisite ceramics in the age-old Portuguese style with delightfully and contemporary designs that lend them an entirely new and modern perspective.

Oficina da Terra and its young entrepreneurial owners have won numerous accolades since being established nearly a decade ago. Oficina da Terra is the place to come to buy real works of art that are more than a class above the usual tourist ceramic fare.

Rua Vasco da Gama and Rua Candido dos Reis are two other interesting shopping spots. Rua Vasco da Gama is home to several independent stores selling a range of wares of interest to the tourist and local resident alike, including a friendly organic health food shop selling vegetarian foods and gluten-free produce as well as some quirky artisan wood products and rugs.

Rua Candido dos Reis has a more upmarket selection including some independent clothing boutiques and a couple of jewellery stores stocking some interesting filigree gold pieces in Portugal's minimum standard 19.2 carat.

For books head to the Livraria Nazareth or the Livraria Som das Letras. The Livraria Nazareth stocks a good selection of maps in its upstairs showroom, including many of the Alentejo and Évora as well as some English novels, while the Livraria Som das Letras has a fair amount of choice in French and English books.

Évora was slow to follow the trend for large-scale mall shopping, but the past few years have seen it catch up with other urban areas with a new retail park and shopping centre. With the main retail park area already open and in operation, the accompanying mall, Évora Shopping, broke ground in late 2011 and is due for inauguration in 2013. With a cinema complex, supermarket and many major high street names set out over 20,000 square metres Évora Shopping is likely to transform the face of shopping in Évora.

Arts & Crafts

As a UNESCO World Heritage site, Évora has plenty of traditional architecture and design to boast about. However, when you scratch beneath the surface of the delightful Roman, Gothic and Romantic buildings, there is a thriving arts and crafts scene in the city that meshes the traditional and the modern with much aplomb.

If you are looking for some interesting mementos of your trip to Évora, either as a gift for a friend or loved one or as a decoration for your home, there is plenty here to choose from to suit all budgets and tastes.

Portugal is renowned for its crafts such as traditional basketware, carved cork wood, ceramics and filigree gold jewellery, as well as for its lace-making and traditional costume making and Évora offers a good selection of each.

Street Markets

Several open-air markets provide the ideal starting point for your discovery of art and craft in Évora. A large-scale open-air market takes place at the Rossio de São Bras, just outside the castle walls, on the second Tuesday of each month.

Here you will find a good selection of crafts including basketware, carved cork wood utensils and decorative figures, traditional costumes and handmade lace bed linen, table linen and decorative items.

The Aqueduct market sees a rotation of four different markets on each Sunday of the month. The Aqueduct market is the place to sift out antiquities, old books, collectables and arts and crafts depending on which Sunday you visit. On busy weekends there may be a lot of tat to sift through but it is often well worth it for some lovely traditional pieces in excellent condition.

Much of the local area in this Alentejo region of south-central Portugal is swathed in cork trees. This attractive wood with its distinctive grain lends itself perfectly to making wooden plates, bowls, utensils, figurines and other objects with either a useful or a decorative purpose.

Many of the pieces are produced out of town in artisan workshops or small factories and brought in for sale in the small craft boutiques hidden away behind the doorways of Évora's ancient city-centre buildings.

Avenida 5 de Outubro is the main shopping street in Évora and home to several such shops, stocking examples that are both intricate and more rustic. Take a stroll down the full length of Avenida 5 de

Outubro to weigh up your many options before you decide to take the plunge and buy.

All Things Ceramics

Portugal has a long history in ceramics and is well-known for its beautiful hand-painted figurines and decorative items as well as its ceramic tiles. While many of Évora's grand buildings display numerous hand-painted tiles with designs of exquisite detail, the modern-day city retains this strong tradition and is home to various ateliers where original works are produced, as well as many shops selling more mainstream versions.

Many of the same shops on the Avenida 5 de Outubro that feature the lovely cork wood accessories are also a good place to find interesting ceramic works. Plates, bowls, cups, vases and a whole host of decorative items can be found here in abundance, featuring both traditional and more modern hand-painted designs.

Lovers of modern arts and crafts, especially those who enjoy ceramics, will adore the Oficina da Terra on the Rua do Raimundo. This ceramics studio and museum is run by two young local artists, Tiago Cabeça and Magda Ventura, and was established nearly a decade ago. The young entrepreneurs have been the proud recipients of many accolades and have been featured extensively in the media both in Portugal and abroad.

This is the place to come for some really original, modern and quirky ceramic works, sculpted and painted with an almost childlike sense of ingénue and yet remarkably sophisticated and original at the same time.

Piéce De Resistance

The Aldeia da Terra is the *piéce de resistance* of the Oficina da Terra team and is not to be missed on your discovery of the Évora crafts scene. This is a permanent exhibition set outside the old city walls, taking the form of a full model village designed in their own individual, quirky style.

The Aldeia da Terra comes complete with famous monuments, whitewashed houses, cars, taxis, bicycles and miniature figures of many townspeople going about their everyday life. The display shows more than a touch of humour and is guaranteed to put a smile on the face of every visitor.

Accommodation

Best Hotels in Evora

The variety of hotels in Évora is one of the major attractions of staying in this historic city. This was one of Portugal's most prominent cities during the sixteenth century and many of its beautiful buildings have remained intact right up to the present day, making the city fully deserving of its designation as a UNESCO World Heritage site.

Accommodation in Évora is varied and interesting, with rooms in converted royal palaces, sixteenth-century stately homes and behind the ancient walls of centuries-old convents. Whatever you are looking for, hotels in Évora are unlikely to disappoint.

The Évora Inn Chiado Design hotel is a living work of art in itself, a place where traditional architectural style and modern aesthetics meet with wonderful effect. Located in a building of historic relevance (where the new Portuguese republic was proclaimed in 1910) it offers a wonderfully contemporary setting from which to enjoy the city. Rooms are surprisingly low priced and there is a dormitory option for those seeking good quality accommodations in Évora at hostel prices.

The Hostel Santantão is centrally located in the Praça do Giraldo, the main square in the centre of town that has played a pivotal role in its history and culture since its heyday in the sixteenth century and, like the Old Évora Hostel located close by, makes a great city-centre base from which to enjoy the city.

There are plenty of good four-star accommodations in Évora. Try the Évora Hotel, located within two hectares of landscaped gardens or, at the other end of the spectrum, the Casa de S. Tiago, the stately home now converted into a boutique hotel with just six beautifully designed and individual rooms. Other options include the Albergaria do Calvario recently remodelled to make the most of the space available within its wonderful sixteenth-century walls, and the Hotel M'AR de Ar Muralhas, which offers spacious gardens of landscaped greenery right within Évora's ancient city walls.

Several of Évora's famous convents have been restored and reopened as five-star boutique hotels. Try the Pousada de Évora, Convento dos Lóios whose luxury guest bedrooms each offer their own style, décor and history, or the fifteenth-century Convento do Espinheiro Hotel & Spa, with 92 rooms and suites decorated in a range of eclectic styles.

The Hotel M'AR de Ar Aqueduto is one of the most luxurious and glamorous hotels in Évora, Portugal. Located in the heart of the historic centre in the building of the sixteenth-century Sepulveda Palace, it retains many of the original architectural features for which this UNESCO World Heritage city has earned its fame. The hotel combines the best of contemporary design and traditional features throughout its 64 rooms, award-winning dining room and luxurious spa.

Convento Do Espinheiro Hotel & Spa

The Convento do Espinheiro Hotel & Spa is located in the building of a fifteenth-century convent in the historic town of Évora, Portugal.

The convent building has been beautifully restored to a level fitting of this UNESCO World Heritage destination and offers guests the perfect base from which to explore the city.

The Convento do Espinheiro Hotel & Spa offers a total of 92 rooms including 5 suites and a breath-taking Royal Suite, decorated in a variety of styles to suit your preference. All offer comfort and luxury as a matter of course, combined with eclectic styles dating anywhere from the fifteenth-century origins of the convent itself through to the quirky styles of 1950s' interior décor.

All rooms come equipped with King size or twin beds, a well-stocked mini-bar, electronic in-room safe, hot-and-cold air conditioning, plasma TV with satellite programming and video on demand and en-suite bathroom with walk-in shower, separate bathtub and complimentary bathrobes and slippers.

Deluxe rooms are available with a variety of views from pool to garden areas, decorated in traditional luxury hotel style, while Heritage rooms offer a real taste of life's finer things in fifteenth-century Portugal and are located right in the ancient convent building with views out to the Don Sebastião Square.

Guests in search of something a little different can opt for the 1950s-inspired design rooms. These are large rooms with a spacious living area and are located in the especially designed new wing of the hotel, offering beautiful views out over the hotel's eight hectares of landscaped greenery. If you really want to push the boat out, opt for a Deluxe suite with fine Bulgari touches or the Royal Suite, named after King John II of Portugal and occupying an impressive 110 square metres with sweeping views from the private terrace right out over the city of Évora.

The Convento do Espinheiro Hotel & Spa occupies one of the largest leisure spaces of any hotel in this area of Portugal. There is a children's playground and mini club to entertain the little ones throughout the day and a gymnasium and spa for the health-conscious.

The hotel has a strong emphasis on health and fitness to maximise on its enviable location in eight hectares of beautiful Évora landscape, the hotel offers an outdoor pool, tennis and paddle facilities with complimentary equipment and bike tours throughout the grounds and local area.

Convento do Espinheiro Hotel & Spa
Portugal
Tel: +351 266 788 200
Email: reservas@conventodoespinheiro.com

Évora Inn Chiado Design

The Évora Inn Chiado Design is the first design hotel to be established in the historic city of Évora in central Portugal.

This UNESCO World heritage city, set within ancient city walls whose face has changed little in centuries, is a must-visit location for visitors keen to explore the historic monuments and architecture of old world Portugal and the Évora

Inn Chiado Design hotel is set right in the heart of the action, on the Rua da Republica overlooking the main square, the Praça de Giraldo.

The Évora Inn Chiado Design hotel opened recently to much acclaim, gaining attention from the travel press not just in Portugal but as far afield as New York and elsewhere. The Chiado Design team have taken a building of historic relevance (where the new Portuguese republic was proclaimed in 1910) and traditional architectural style, and located within it a living work of modern art that embraces both the building's colourful past and its Technicolor future.

Behind the unassuming period walls lies a world of white walls, modern designer furniture and bold colour schemes, creating an environment that is unmatched anywhere in Évora.

The communal areas include a shared kitchen area, a reading and internet area and a lounge in which a small art gallery is located. The hotel boasts several family rooms and double rooms in addition to a low-cost area for up to 22 people in dormitory-style accommodation but make no mistake, this is shared sleeping with a touch of class!

The rooms are ingeniously named to conjure up the very sense of their history and design aesthetic. Choose from "Exuberance", "Nostalgia", "Live Life", "Stars", "Pop", "Diamonds", "Revolution", "Soft Portuguese", "Travelling" and "Lucy in the Sky", the terrace room located right at the top of the building.

There is no elevator on the premises so if you prefer to save your legs for the sightseeing it is worth requesting a room on the lower floors;

however, the higher floors do offer some lovely views out across the square and city spires that make the extra legwork worthwhile.

The kitchen area is suitable for preparing snacks and simple meals, however there is a small café located right beneath the hotel serving excellent snacks and a hearty breakfast, perfect for setting you up for a long day touring the sights of the historic city of Évora.

Évora Inn Chiado Design
Rua da República, 11
Évora, Portugal
Tel: +351 266 744 500
Mob: +351 962 216 272
Email: mail@Évorainn.com

Old Évora Hostel

The Old Évora Hostel is centrally located in the historic city of Évora, Portugal, midway between the famous Praça do Giraldo, centrepiece of this ancient town since it came to prominence back in the sixteenth century, and the bus station at which many of the town's visitors arrive for the first time.

All the major tourist attractions are within a walk from the Old Évora Hostel, including the Capela dos Ossos, the ancient city walls that encircle the historic sites of this UNESCO World Heritage city, and the churches and convents that have stood within the city limits for centuries.

The rooms are well-equipped with hair dryer, ironing board, in-room personal safe and microwave, making it the perfect location for travellers on a budget who prefer to save their funds for splashing out away from their hotel walls rather than within them. Luxurious it may not be, but with rooms starting at around fifteen euros per night, this is the ultimate in decent quality budget accommodation.

This is a place to make friends and share your experiences with your fellow guests in the TV lounge and shared kitchen. Facilities for individuals also include wireless internet throughout, mobile phone charging, luggage storage, security lockers, reading bed lights, iron and ironing board, free linen, use of hair dryer and a hearty breakfast every morning.

The friendly staff are helpful and eager to ensure their guests get the most out of their stay in this attractive town in the Ribatejo region of Portugal. They will happily provide advice on local attractions, getting out and about, and the best times to visit the various historical sites.

There is so much to do away from Évora's city walls too, such as adventuring, hiking, mountain biking, sightseeing biking, horse riding, abseiling and even hot air ballooning that guests staying at the Old Évora Hostel will be spoilt for choice when deciding how to spend their days. The tourist office is just a three-minute walk away and is well worth a visit to find out everything that is offered during your stay.

For good quality budget accommodation in the historic city of Évora in central Portugal, this is an excellent choice.

Old Évora Hostel
Rua Serpa Pinto / Travessa do Barão nº 4 A
7000-556
Évora, Portugal
Tel: +351 934 734 493
Email: oldevorahostel@gmail.com

Albergaria Do Calvario

The Albergaria do Calvario is conveniently located close to the Central of Évora, Portugal, within the ancient city walls. The hotel is a four-star property run on a bed and breakfast basis and provides the perfect place for a comfortable and cosy hotel stay in this delightful city.

The Albergaria do Calvario was completely remodelled in 2008 to provide even better quality accommodation within its sixteenth-century buildings, which were originally constructed and used as an olive oil mill to serve the neighbouring convent. The hotel has twenty rooms and three suites set out across two floors, each well-equipped with hot and cold air conditioning, en-suite marble bathrooms fitted with hair dryer, television with cable programming, direct dial telephone, free Wi-Fi, and an in-room security safe. Rooms contain twin or double beds and are particularly spacious. One room is also adapted for wheelchair users.

The Albergaria do Calvario offers a sumptuous buffet breakfast each day, which can be taken in the cheerful breakfast room or outside on the terrace during high season. The emphasis on locally-grown produce and fresh baking, setting you up perfectly for a day of sightseeing in one of Portugal's most historic cities.

Freshly prepared fruit juices and smoothies, delicious wholegrain breads and rich cakes abound, along with cheese and ham brought in directly from farms in Évora and the surrounding area.

The hotel bar has an extensive and well-chosen wine list, perfect for selecting a bottle to enjoy at sundown on the terrace with your travel partners or other guests staying at this friendly establishment and the lunch time and evening menus offer plenty of choice for everyone. Room service is also available 24 hours a day for guests to enjoy breakfast, drinks or snacks in the privacy of their own space.

This is a hotel where the staff takes great pride in knowing each of their guests by name, greeting them as they would members of their own family and ensuring they want for nothing during their stay.

Car parking is available beneath the hotel and it is well located for exploring all the sights of the ancient city of Évora, Portugal, on foot

Albergaria do Calvario
Travessa dos Lugares, 3
7000-565 Évora, Portugal
Tel: +351 266 745 930
Fax: +351 266 745 939
Email: hotel@albergariadocalvario.com

Casa De S. Tiago

There is little doubt that the best location for visitors to stay when visiting Évora in Portugal is right in the heart of the historic city centre. This bewitching city sits within the limits of the ancient stone walls that encircle it and it is here at its heart that the Casa de S. Tiago is located.

The Casa de S. Tiago is a comfortable boutique hotel set in a carefully restored period house dating back to the sixteenth century, during the reign of Don Manuel I of Portugal, when Évora was in its heyday. Guests staying here will feel themselves swept back in time to the Portugal of a bygone age, understanding how it would have felt to live centuries ago in this city that is now a UNESCO World Heritage site.

The aristocratic exterior, with its sculpted portico and covered entrance with intricate stonework embellishments add a sense of grandeur to the building that make you feel as though you have come home to somewhere very special.

The Casa de S. Tiago comprises just six rooms along with some lovely communal areas. In true boutique style, each room is decorated individually with its own period style. All are en-suite as you would expect of a hotel of this calibre, with separate shower and bathtub, and come equipped with hot and cold air conditioning and television. Newspapers are delivered daily to each room and room service is available 24 hours a day for guests' comfort.

There is a bar, sitting room and attractive garden to enable guests to enjoy their downtime even after their busy days of sightseeing come to an end and general hotel services include laundry and dry cleaning, valet parking and a business centre to ensure guests can keep up to date with their colleagues, friends and family members.

The hotel is the perfect jumping-off point for exploring the many monuments and historic buildings that are dotted throughout the "museum city" of Évora. The Capela dos Ossos and the Praça do Giraldo are situated within an easy walk from your front door and unusual destinations such as the Roman baths are just outside town.

So relax, enjoy a sumptuous buffet breakfast and allow yourself to be transported back in time as you visit some of Portugal's most exciting historic sites.

Casa de S. Tiago
Largo Alexandre Herculano, 2
7000-501 Évora, Portugal
Tel: +351 266702686
Fax: +351 266702686
Email: fvasconcelos@casasaotiago.com

Évora Hotel

Évora Hotel is a good-sized four-star hotel located within two hectares of landscaped gardens in the historic town of Évora, Portugal. This hotel is the ideal choice for family groups and couples looking to explore the UNESCO World Heritage sites close by or indulge in all manner of outdoor pursuits and adventure sports in the surrounding areas. It is also popular with business guests who are well catered for with the hotel's meeting and conference facilities.

The Évora Hotel offers 170 rooms comprised of standard, superior and junior suite formats, all offering views out over the landscaped gardens, rolling hills or pool areas. Each room comes complete with hot-and-cold air conditioning, internet, television with satellite programming, a well-stocked minibar, in-room safety deposit box, direct dial telephone, hair dryer and private balcony with views.

Superior rooms offer a little more room, marble bathrooms and even more impressive views thanks to their location on the upper floors, while the junior suites boast a separate living area, making them perfect for families travelling together, especially those with young children. For something special, request the Évora Suite, a spacious area with separate bedroom and sitting room, marble bathroom with hydro-massage bath and three separate private balconies.

The Évora hotel is a great option for families not just because of its flexible accommodation options but also thanks to its on-site kids' club. Here the young ones are entertained by qualified staff who dedicate their working hours to ensuring their charges' safety and enjoyment, leaving their parents free to enjoy a few precious hours relaxing around the pool area or out and about in Évora, exploring the sights of this historic city.

There is a whole range of activities designed to keep the little ones entertained, from painting and team games to sporting activities such as tennis and climbing, plus of course supervised fun and games in the children's shallow outdoor pool.

The Évora Hotel's in-house is perfect for keeping in shape during your stay in Portugal. Take a workout in the health and fitness centre before retreating to the spa treatment area for a relaxing dip in the jacuzzi.

The Sol Poente Restaurant serves the best of Portugal's traditional cuisine from the local Alentejo region along with a few stars on the menu such as the shark soup. Several set menus are on offer to enable guests so savour a little of everything that the restaurant has to offer.

Évora Hotel
Av. Túlio Espanca
7002-502 Évora

Portugal
Tel: +351 266 748 800
Email: reservas@evorahotel.pt

M'ar De Ar Aqueduto

The Hotel M'AR de Ar Aqueduto is one of the most luxurious and glamorous hotels in Évora, Portugal. Located in the heart of the historic centre in the building of the sixteenth-century Sepulveda Palace, it retains many of the original architectural features for which this UNESCO World Heritage city has earned its fame.

The hotel combines the best of contemporary design and traditional features throughout its 64 rooms, award-winning dining room and luxurious spa. The sophisticated guest rooms are beautifully furnished with an eclectic mix of period pieces with a modern twist. All feature en-suite bathrooms with robes, slippers and hair dryer as well as hot-and-cold air conditioning, direct dial telephone, internet, LCD HD television, safety deposit box and well-stocked minibar.

Classic rooms offer the additional comfort of a desk and sitting area with sofa and guests can even choose a spa room, located right in the Spa Aqueduto, where couples can receive their spa treatments in the comfort of their own rooms, equipped with shower and circular hydro massage tub and wide private terrace area facing the orange orchard.

Common areas at the Hotel M'AR de Ar Aqueduto include a gourmet restaurant, a reading room with computers and internet access, meeting and conference rooms for up to 200 guests, a spa and a lovely outdoor pool in a unique setting with the beautiful aqueduct as its backdrop.

Services for guests' convenience include local area tours, 24-hour room service, airport transfers, washing and dry cleaning services and bicycle rental to enable guests to get the most out of their visit to Évora.

The Hotel M'AR de Ar Aqueduto is one of the most sought-after hotels in this area of Portugal not just for its accommodation, location and ambience but also for its gourmet restaurant, the Degust'AR. Award-winning chef Antonio Nobre has published several well-known recipe books and is often seen on Portuguese television presenting and guest featuring on various cookery programmes.

His cookery embraces the aromatic flavours of the Alentejo region with its pig rearing and olive growing traditions, bringing a modern European twist to centuries-old recipes.

Located on the ground floor of this former palace building the dining room is a study in grandeur and period architecture and worth a visit wherever you are staying on your visit to Évora, Portugal.

M'AR de Ar Aqueduto
Rua Cândido dos Reis 72
7000 Évora, Portugal
Tel: +351 266 740 700
Fax: + 351 266 740 735
Email: reservas@mardearhotels.com

M'ar De Ar Muralhas

The Hotel M'AR de Ar Muralhas is located in the historic centre of Évora within the UNESCO World Heritage area of this famous city in Portugal. It is just a five-minute walk from the Praça do Giraldo, which has been considered the very heart of the city since the times of the sixteenth century.

This four-star hotel is set within spacious gardens of landscaped greenery within Évora's ancient city walls, providing plenty of room for guests to relax and enjoy some downtime no matter how busy their sightseeing schedules are.

The Hotel M'AR de Ar Muralhas is comprised of 85 rooms with double or twin beds and six suites including the extravagant and supremely comfortable Royal Suite. The rooms are decorated according to several themes, with the classic rooms featuring a rustic finish and light furnishings. All include a desk and chair, hot-and-cold air conditioning, direct-dial telephone, cable internet connection, LCD HD television, minibar, hair dryer and complimentary bathroom accessories.

Superior doubles are located on the first floor and feature wide terraces with exterior furniture and plush furnishings, while the suites are larger, with a separate seating area and sofa and offer a variety of views either over the walls and hotel gardens or across the city of Évora.

If you are looking to push the boat out and indulge in luxury during your trip to Portugal, book yourself into the Royal Suite on the second floor. This spacious accommodation includes two bedrooms, a living room and a bathroom with hydro-massage bath and separate shower cubicle.

The gardens at the Hotel M'AR de Ar Muralhas are set with swimming pool and a poolside bar, which is lit up at night to create a delightful ambience under the stars of the Alentejo region of central Portugal. Enjoy an aperitif here before making your way into the restaurant of acclaimed chef Antonio Nobre.

Antonio looks after the restaurant both at the Hotel M'AR de Ar Muralhas and at its sister hotel the Hotel M'AR de Ar Aqueduto and is well known in Portugal for his many published cookery books and his regular appearances on national television.

Sabores do Alentejo restaurant features Alentejo cuisine with a Mediterranean twist, mixing the flavours of the two regions to great effect. Breakfast is served here on a buffet breakfast every morning, setting you up perfectly for a day of sightseeing and activity in the local area.

M'AR de Ar Muralhas
Travessa da Palmeira, 4/6
7000-546 Évora, Portugal
Tel.: + 351 266 739 300
Fax: + 351 266 739 305
Email: reservas@mardearhotels.com

Pousada De Évora Convento Dos Lóios

Pousada de Évora, Convento dos Lóios is set in a former convent and is one of the most famous and well-preserved architectural buildings in the historic city of Évora, Portugal. The historic centre of Évora is classified as a UNESCO World Heritage site and attracts visitors throughout the year to wander through the ancient streets and explore the hidden secrets of this mystical and beautiful city.

The Pousada de Évora, Convento dos Lóios was restored and opened as a pousada in 1965, the rooms beautifully converted into luxury guest bedrooms, each with its own style, décor, and history. The renovation has remained sympathetic to the original purpose, style and architecture of the convent and in each and every square metre there is a reminder of its rich past.

Each room in this luxury hotel is equipped with hot-and-cold air conditioning, television with cable programming, mini bar, en-suite bathroom with hairdryer and complimentary bathrobes, telephone, in-room safety deposit box and internet connection.

The public areas include a spacious bar and lounge where guests can relax and share their stories after a day of sightseeing in this beautiful town of central Portugal, free Wi-Fi throughout, a restaurant and large outdoor swimming pool in the hotel grounds.

The restaurant is open for breakfast, lunch and dinner, with breakfast served in continental buffet style. Room service is also available for guests who would prefer to enjoy their meal within the privacy of their own room. The restaurant serves delicious traditional dishes from regional Portugal and offers private dining for small groups or business meetings as well as the open restaurant space.

Business guests are well taken care of with meeting rooms and audio visual facilities, ensuring that this hotel is as popular with business guests as it is with couples and family groups.

The staff at the Pousada de Évora, Convento dos Lóios are friendly and welcoming and happy to help guests organise a range of activities in the local area. In addition to sightseeing in the historic town of Évora, there is plenty of hiking, horse riding, mountain biking, shooting, and evening hot air ballooning for an entirely different perspective on the rolling green terrain.

Pousada de Évora, Convento dos Lóios
Largo Conde Vila-Flor
7000-804 Évora, Portugal
Tel: +351 266 730 070
Fax: +351 266 707 248
Email: guest@pousadas.pt

Useful Information

Useful Contacts

Évora is a popular tourist town located in south central Portugal, some 130 kilometres from the capital city of Lisbon. The town offers many privately run amenities aimed at ensuring travellers from all over the world are able to enjoy it to the full. It is also well furnished with a full range of public services.

For travel information to and from Evora, see the following services and links:

Transport information: www.transpor.pt `SEP`

ACP- Automobile club in Portugal: www.acp.pt `SEP`

Brisa National Motorway Network Company: www.brisa.pt `SEP`

CP- Comboios de Portugal (Portuguese Train): www.cp.pt

The Évora Tourist Information Office is located at:
Praça do Giraldo, 73
Tel: +351 266 777 071
www2.cm-evora.pt/guiaturistico/

The staff speaks English, French and Spanish and the office provides maps, restaurant listings and public phones. The wheelchair-accessible office is open daily from May to October, 9am to 7pm and from November to April, 9am to 6pm.

Self-guided audio tours of the city are €2, returnable before 5.30pm.

We hope that once you arrive in Evora, your time will be taken up exploring the wonderful churches, monasteries and Roman remains. However, in the unlikely event that you require them, we have put together the following useful telephone numbers for Évora's main public services:

National emergency number: 112
Évora Police

Local Police: Rua Francisco Soares Lusitano

Tel: +351 266 70 20 22

PSP- Policia de Segurança Pública: www.psp.pt

GNR- Guarda Nacional Repúblicana: www.gnr.pt

Évora Hospitals
Hospital do Espírito Santo

Lg. Senhor Jesus da Pobreza

Located near city wall and the intersection with R.

Dr. Augusto Eduardo Nunes

Tel: +351 266 74 01 00 or 266 75 84 24

Pharmacy Farmácia Galeno

Rua da República, 34

+351 266 70 32 77

Open Monday to Friday, 9am-1pm and 3-7pm.

Post Office
Rua de Olivença

Tel: +351 266 74 54

How to Get to Evora

The municipality and city of Évora are located more or less due east from Lisbon in central Portugal. Most visitors arriving in Portugal from overseas will arrive in the capital before making their onward journey from Lisbon to Evora.

The journey from Lisbon to Évora is relatively straightforward whichever transport method you choose. Évora directions by car are simplest if you take the A2 by either bridge, before switching onto the A6 then finally the N114 following the Évora directions. It is around 140 kilometres from Lisbon to Évora, and another popular way of making the journey is by bus, for which a round-trip bus ticket costs around 10 euros for students and 12 euros full price.

For information about how to get to Évora by train, check the internet for the latest times as these can be subject to change. The trip takes one hour and twenty minutes and the station is just ten minutes walk from the centre of town when you arrive.

If you are wondering how to get to Évora from starting destinations other than Lisbon, it is just as straightforward. Travel from Porto is very easy by car down the main A1 motorway, before joining the A2 and following directions from Lisbon. It is also possible to arrive in Portugal from continental

Europe, with the Spain-Portugal crossing at Ayamonte, via Seville, proving to be the most popular route.

By train (distance: 130 km): There are 4 trains to Evora daily (5 trains on Sundays). The trip takes 1h20 and it's a very comfortable train. The Évora train station is located close to the city center (around 10 min walking). You can check the timetable of trains in the official website of Comboios de Portugal.

Get around: one of the nicer ways to see the city is by horse carriage ride. You can find them near the Cathedral.

Otherwise there's no real problem in walking between most of the main sights.

Weather in Évora

The weather in Évora contributes enormously to the popularity of this UNESCO World Heritage city.

Évora is located in the Alentejo region of Portugal, in the southern central zone of the country and enjoys one of the best climates in the country.

Évora weather is dry and very warm through the summer months, especially during July and August, however the summer season is lovely and long as a result usually stretching from early May to the end of September. There is very little rainfall during this period; however the nights are usually still cool enough to ensure a good night's sleep.

Spring and autumn are popular times to visit Portugal and Evora is no exception. The weather in Évora remains mostly dry during the early and late season months, and if you enjoy taking part in adventure sports or doing a lot of sightseeing on foot, the slightly cooler air makes this an excellent proposition.

Most of Évora's rainfall comes during the winter months. This is when the city is at its quietest and therefore ideal if you are looking to avoid the high season crowds.

One of the reasons that make the Alentejo region popular when in Portugal is the hot weather and comfortable cool winters. And Évora is the place to prove it. Even though the city is relatively far from the south west coast, you will soon forget the sandy beaches, and be overwhelmed by the immensity of a beautiful sunset in the town centre. Évora is particularly peaceful in the spring, especially March through May. Being located in the hottest region in the country, you can expect high temperature and dry weather during the summer.

July and mostly August are the months with the warmest temperature, making your holiday an extremely hot one at this time of year. Despite the heat, you will find yourself enjoying long summer days by taking a quiet walk, or as you dine a traditional meal of tomato soup and lamb stew as late afternoon approaches.

Luckily for many travellers who are big fans of sunny weather, Évora maintains quite a warm climate from May to September. You will probably find more tourists visiting the city between the months of June and September, in comparison to the spring and winter seasons. During the fall the city becomes very intimate and especially involving because of its captivating setting.

In the winter you will find Évora to be cold and rainy. A lesser amount of tourists are seen, and the streets are more deserted. However, this ambience will give you a different look upon the town, and is great for those whom prefer to blend in with the locals and see the city through different eyes.

On a lazy summer afternoon or on a cold winter night in Evora, a taste of the very famed and high quality red wine is a must. Herdade do Esporão and J. Portugal Ramos are two of the top red wines of the region. No matter what the weather is like, there will always be room for a divine meal that will make you beg for more, each time. Based mainly on bread and meats, the gastronomy found in Evora is also known for its cheese, almond sweets, and soups.

From site seeing, to eating typical food and sipping some fabulous red wine, every time seems like the best time to visit Evora.

The End

Made in the USA
Las Vegas, NV
02 March 2025

18932149R00111